MW01277959

"...both he and his wife, Virginia, spent hours with me perfecting my role [in Fly Away Home*]."* –Montgomery Clift

"I must also tell you that I, and many other young actresses and the elite of New York's young debutantes of that era, were among those who kissed your portrait outside the theatre." –Mary Pickford

"...all I wanted was to stand side stage each night to see you, Donny, dancing around in those skin tight trousers..." –Mae West

"I must tell you, I consider Donald Brian to be the greatest performer ever to appear on the Broadway stage." –Lillian Russell

"[Donald Brian] is tireless and surely the most wonderful dancer in the United States." –Wendy Blackmore

"...it would be fair to say that Donny Brian is entirely responsible for all the money I have earned in Hollywood..." –W.C. Fields

Donald Brian, left, with a very youthful Bob Hope, second right, Allan Jenkins and Martha Raye in *Give Me A Sailor* filmed at Paramount Studios in 1939.

DONALD BRIAN

the KING of BROADWAY

Charles Foster

Foreword by Paul O'Neill

Breakwater Books Ltd.

Breakwater Books Ltd.
100 Water Street • P.O. Box 2188 • St. John's • NL • A1C 6E6
www.breakwaterbooks.com

Library and Archives Canada Cataloguing in Publication

Foster, Charles, 1923-
Donald Brian : The King of Broadway / Charles Foster.

Includes index.
ISBN 1-55081-214-9

1. Brian, Donald, 1877-1948. 2. Actors--Canada--Biography.
I. Title.

PN2287.B688F67 2005 792'.02'8092 C2005-906140-5

Design & Layout: Rhonda Molloy Editor: Tamara Reynish

We acknowledge the financial support of The Canada Council for the Arts for our publishing activities.

We acknowledge the financial support of the Government of Canada through the Book Publishing Industry Development Program (BPIDP) for our publishing activities.

Printed in Canada

Contents

Foreword

Donald Brian, the Broadway star, who was born in St. John's, recalls that his voice was first raised in song in the Roman Catholic Church, he and his mother attended during his childhood. He also took part in a Benevolent Irish Society concert in 1880, on the stage of St. Patrick's Hall in St. John's, singing *All On Account of Liza* and *Little Widow Dunn.* How he became known as the "King of Broadway" 27 years later in New York is a remarkable, success story that is told on the pages of this biography. He was perhaps the most famous Newfoundlander (worldwide) who ever lived, with the possible exception of John Murray Anderson, whom the *N.Y. Times* saluted when he died with the headline "Uncle Broadway is Dead." Both men were famous headliners in American show business and share the same fate, that of being almost entirely forgotten in their home town.

Born in St. John's in 1875 at 3 Queen St., now the site of a tavern, his mother was Margaret Selby, and his father, Donald Francis Brian, Superintendent of the St. John's Street and Bridge Department. Following the little lad's BIS concert, he was in demand among St. John's music circles. His father died suddenly January 3, 1883. Margaret, a talented seamstress, provided for herself and her son by sewing. When her friend Molly (O'Malley) Reichert came home from Boston on a visit in 1893, she urged Margaret to go back with her to the New England city where seamstresses were in great demand. Donald protested strenuously, wanting to stay in St. John's, but Molly prevailed. The two women and 18 year-old Donald sailed from St. John's on a ship laden with a cargo of fish, which he later described as a "smelly fish boat."

My mother, who lived in New York City in the mid-20s and worked as a governess with several wealthy families, was a theatre addict, who often talked to me as a boy about shows she had seen on Broadway, especially such musicals as *Rose Marie, Countess Maritza, The Student Prince* and *Rio Rita.* She could even sing a song or two from each of them. I loved to hear them and when I showed an interest she told me of seeing Donald Brian on Broadway, and that I should be proud of him because he was from St. John's. It came as an eye-opener to me that someone from St. John's was a Broadway star!

As a boy, when not spending my afternoons in the library, I was sitting in the dentist's chair, getting endless temporary fillings, a fad of the time, from Dr. Mogue Power, who lived three doors away from us on Cochrane Street and knew my parents well. He told me on one occasion to tell my mother he had been to New York and met with Donald Brian during his visit. I was amazed Dr. Power knew the star, just as he was amazed I knew who he was talking about. As he drilled a tooth with his foot-pumped drill, he said the actor was one of his best friends as a boy. They had gone to school together and kept up their friendship. He also told me Brian came home once on a visit, where he was treated with kindness but, with an anonymity, which he enjoyed, from the press and the public in his hometown. According to Dr. Power, he had a great love for this city, and left, never to return. The story of that visit is compellingly told in this biography.

When it was announced an Arts and Culture Centre was to be built in St. John's as the Federal Government's contribution to Canada's 1967 centennial celebrations, I wrote a letter to Premier Smallwood suggesting the centre be called the John Murray Anderson Centre and the theatre the Donald Brian Theatre, to honour two of Newfoundland's greatest sons. All I received in reply was a two line acknowledgment of receipt signed J.R. Smallwood and, sadly, nothing was ever done about the suggestion, yet the Provincial Government named the library in the Centre for Dr. A.C. Hunter of Memorial University, an outstanding man and truly meritorious professor.

Those who have heard of Donald Brian and know of his remarkable career, as well as those who know nothing about him, will find this biography as absorbing as it is informative. Charles Foster's telling of the life of the King of Broadway is a worthy tribute to a man who achieved greatness as a performer on stage and in film, but who for some reason was forgotten in his own city and country, both of which he loved dearly. Perhaps this autobiography may even move the Provincial Government to name the still unnamed Centre and Theatre in memory of two Newfoundlanders who are now regarded as immortals of American show business.

Paul O'Neill
St. John's, Newfoundland and Labrador, Canada
2005

Prologue

Dear Reader:

It was my good fortune, in 1943, to meet Donald Brian and his beautiful wife, Virginia O'Brien, in Hollywood. Following a serious illness, I was on leave from my pilot training with the British Royal Air Force in Calgary, Canada, and had been invited to spend my vacation at the home of Sidney Olcott and his wife, Valentine, on Bedford Drive in Beverly Hills.

Canadian-born Sid Olcott, one of the great directors of the silent film era in both New York and Hollywood, had first interested Donald Brian in the fledgling film industry in the early 1900s when Brian was working on the Broadway stage and Olcott was making silent films in New York.

When I arrived in Hollywood in July 1943, it was a Tuesday night tradition that Sid Olcott and others, like Charlie Chaplin and Mary Pickford, who got more pleasure from the silent era than from the new sound age, met at Olcott's home to relive the days they loved as they watched the superb silent films that they, and others, had enjoyed making, or appearing in, decades earlier.

The night after I arrived in Hollywood the Olcotts had invited Donald Brian and his wife Virginia to join in the fun because Sid Olcott had put together dozens of snippets of the films that Donald had appeared in for the Kalem Company many years earlier in New York.

Jose Iturbi, the brilliant concert and film pianist, also a Bedford Drive resident, attended each session and played piano accompaniment to the silent films. Iturbi told me he started his career playing piano for silent films and loved the opportunity of reviving those wonderful days.

Another invited guest was Montreal-born Douglas Shearer, the man who put an end to silent films when he created, for Metro-Goldwyn-Mayer, the equipment that made sound and film synchronisation possible.

Douglas Shearer had also invented the wire recorder, forerunner of today's tape recorder. His bulky machine weighed about thirty pounds and had a coated wire that wound from one reel to the other. This remarkable wire machine was able to record the human voice so well it was uncanny.

Shearer heard me asking hundreds of questions of the stars I met. He saw me scribble notes in dozens of notebooks that quickly became full.

"Charlie," he said, "you'll never be able to remember half the things you are being told and those scribbled notes are going to be very difficult to decipher. I'm going to lend you my wire recorder. Every night I will have one of the secretaries from MGM pick up the reel you have used and replace it with a new unused roll.

"The secretary, Ann Howard, has Louis B. Mayer's approval to spend the night transcribing every word you capture on the recorder and she will leave a typewritten copy with each new roll of wire."

Because of Doug Shearer's amazing wire recorder the book you are about to read became possible. I recorded more than four hours of conversations with Donald Brian and his wife Virginia O'Brien. I had no idea then how I would use the fascinating tales I collected from them, but I have always loved asking questions, a habit that has provided me with a lucrative career for more decades than I care to remember.

My first book in 2000, *Stardust and Shadows*, about the silent film era, included a chapter on Sid Olcott. That chapter brought me an interesting letter from Denise Brian of Houston, Texas. "I remember Sid Olcott and his delightful wife Val," she wrote. "In fact I remember meeting you once at the Olcotts home when my mother and father dropped by for a visit. My father was Donald Brian, once a very important star on Broadway, and my mother was actress Virginia O'Brien who was also very successful in theatre until I came along and she decided to retire.

"I know you used a wire recorder to interview my parents at our home on Bedford Drive, and wonder if any of those interview transcriptions still exist.

"Hundreds of things were written about my parents in newspaper and magazine articles in the period from the early 1900s to around 1943 when father was nearing the end of his career.

"I have read and reread those stories and wonder how many were true or how many were just publicity stories. I have often wondered what dad and mother actually said in their own words. I would give anything to read the transcripts that you were given before you left Hollywood.

"I was only fifteen when we met, and often wondered what happened to you in World War II. It is satisfying now to know you survived. Father sold the Bedford Drive house early in 1944 and we all returned to our home in Great Neck near New York. Sadly I lost touch with the Olcotts a few years later.

"Nobody ever wrote a book about my father's very successful career on Broadway and the fun he had later in Hollywood. I have always been puzzled why nobody thought him, and mother, worthwhile subjects for a book. Even now when I visit theatre friends in New York they still talk about Donald Brian and Virginia O'Brien."

I was able to send Denise Brian photocopies of the 109 pages that Ann Howard transcribed from the conversations we held almost sixty years earlier. In return Denise sent me a number of programs from the shows in which Donald and Virginia starred, and several photographs including an autographed photograph of her father, which she said was the last one in her possession.

This is the real story of Donald Brian and all the people he helped on their way to stardom. I think it will make you proud to know that he came from St. John's, Newfoundland and never lost his love for the city of his birth. I hope it will make Denise Brian very proud of both her parents.

Charles Foster
Riverview, New Brunswick, Canada
2005

1 Nothing but Praise

Fred Astaire, one of the world's most celebrated stage, film and television dancers, told the *New York Times* that Donald Brian was undoubtedly the most graceful and elegant dancer ever to appear on the Broadway stage.

Bob Hope said he had created his own easy, relaxed, personality that made him one of the most enduring stars in the world of entertainment, from the technique used by Donald Brian throughout his long career.

Charles Ebbets, builder of Ebbets Field in Flatbush, Brooklyn, in 1913, and boss of the famed Brooklyn Dodgers who played baseball there for forty-four years before moving to Los Angeles, said if Donald Brian had not been such a big star on Broadway, earning ten times the salaries paid to baseball players in the early 1900s, he could easily have earned a regular place on the Dodgers team as a hitter.

In 1925, a few months before he died, Ebbets said this to the *New York Post*: "I once tried to sign Donald Brian to a contract with the Dodgers in 1915 as a publicity stunt, and it made front page news in all the New York daily newspapers, but though he was good enough to make the team he never actually played for us. We couldn't afford him."

George M. Cohan, singer, dancer, composer, producer and director, perhaps the most important and lasting of all Broadway personalities, who discovered Donald Brian in Boston, said he sometimes regretted helping him become a star on Broadway because whenever they appeared together Brian always stole every scene and received the most applause.

Cohan wrote in his autobiography: "Throughout my entire career, considering all my own successes, I have never before or since seen such an outpouring of love for a performer as I experienced on Monday, October 21, 1907, at the New Amsterdam Theatre on 42nd Street in New York City. It was the night Donald Brian made his first appearance as Prince Danilo in *The Merry Widow*, one of the greatest musicals ever staged on Broadway."

Donald Brian, like Cohan, a man of many talents, singer, dancer, actor, teacher and baseball player, first saw the light of day on February 17, 1875, in St. John's, Newfoundland.

He learned the art of tap dancing, singing and stage movement in St. John's, but it was almost 2,000 miles away in New York City where he reached the ultimate pinnacle of his illustrious career when the *New York Times* crowned him, in 1907, "The King of Broadway" after his enormous success playing Prince Danilo in *The Merry Widow*.

Despite the adulation bestowed on him on Broadway in New York and later successes in Hollywood, he never forgot St. John's. He told the *New York Post* in 1923: "If I had my choice of any place in the world in which to live it would be the city in which I was born, St. John's, Newfoundland."

He added: "The warmth of the people, the help and friendliness offered to anyone in need and the total peace and tranquility of the community will never be matched by any other place on earth."

But Donald Brian only returned home to St. John's once. In 1926, the sight of the city in which he was born moved him so much that he told the *New York Times*: "It was like returning to heaven."

Many years later his wife, actress Virginia O'Brien, who accompanied him home on that trip in 1926 for their honeymoon, recalled the visit. "We had travelled in remarkable comfort on a Newfoundland fishing trawler that Donny had arranged to pick us up in Boston and take us to his hometown.

"Donny was always an emotional person, and he found it easy to laugh or cry at whatever situation faced him. As we neared the harbour of St. John's he stood in the prow of the vessel and wept uncontrollably. His entire body shook and when I put my arms around him he said, 'Everything is fine. I am fine. These are tears for a great and joyous moment. I am home again.'

"It was almost thirty years since he had left his home in St. John's, and the trip we made to his birthplace became as memorable to me as it was to him. I was able to see him as a small boy again, living a wonderful life, as we walked around the cobbled streets together.

"If there was any disappointment on that trip it was when he knocked on the door of his old home and nobody answered. But on the way back to New York he told me, 'I am glad nobody was home. I don't think I could have accepted anyone other than my mother opening the door.'"

2 Life in St. John's

Life in St. John's was good for Donald Francis Brian Sr. and his wife, the former Margaret Selby, when Donald Brian Jr. arrived on February 17, 1875, in the front downstairs room of their wood-framed house overlooking the harbour. On hand were a midwife and the local doctor.

Years later, in 1912, Margaret Brian recalled to the *New York Post* that it was an easy delivery. "I like to think the loud noise Donald made in the small parlour that had been converted to a delivery room, because it was close to hot water supplies in the kitchen, was an omen of the wonderful voice he later gave to the world. And dare I suggest that the way he waved his tiny feet in the air that day was perhaps a prelude to the dancing skills that later made him a star on Broadway."

Donald Brian's father was Superintendent of the St. John's Street and Bridge Department, with a salary not magnificent, but sufficient to allow the family to enjoy all of life's necessities.

The Brian's home was just across the street from the waterfront and from a very early age, he estimated at around five, Donald Brian used to run across the road to help the fishermen unload their catches on the wharf.

"I was never paid, but I remember one captain giving me a penny when I rather cleverly caught a fish that somehow went off track when it was thrown to the men on shore," he told the *New York World* in 1910.

"Mostly I was paid in fish and ran home across the road with my arms full. We had an icebox into which they were carefully packed and for days we ate fish for breakfast, lunch and dinner. If mother heard of people having a difficult time making ends meet she would invite them to join us for dinner. My father would set up a second table in the dining room and sometimes we had as many as eight extra guests join us for a hearty meal."

The Brians made a lot of friends through their generosity and when the household was shocked by the sudden death, following an unexpected heart attack, of Donald Brian Sr., in 1883, their generosity was repaid many times over.

"Our home was never short of food," said Donald Brian in Hollywood in 1943. "One of the families we had helped in the past had become very successful and the father of the family had become mayor of St. John's. I can't remember his name now, but clearly remember that he helped ease our pain and made sure we were never in need."

The mayor found Margaret Brian a job with a company that made women's clothing. "She was a great seamstress and had made all our clothing, including my father's suits before he died," he said.

"I was offered the job of manager within weeks of starting work, but I just loved fashioning the clothes so I declined the offer," said Mrs. Brian in 1922 to the *New York Times*.

Though the money was good and friends never neglected them, Donald Brian recalled, in 1943, "We ate a lot of fish in those days. I used to fish in the harbour off the quay while I was waiting for mother to come home from work. There were a lot of fish in those days and in an hour, I could fill my bucket with enough for us and all the neighbours."

The Brian family members were staunch Roman Catholics. "It was the choir director at the church, Herbert O'Sullivan, who first heard me sing in the pew I shared with my mother when I was only eight. He invited me to join the church choir and, as a voice teacher in the city, offered to train my voice free of charge. I owe a great deal to his generosity. I was a soloist when I was ten with a city choral group and in the church choir, both of which he directed. We appeared at many functions, from concerts to weddings and important funerals, even outdoor concerts in the park which were never cancelled even when it rained so hard we could hardly see the audience."

Donald Brian's feet began to tap around the same time. "William 'Billy' Ryan, my best friend in the church choir, had a father, Dennis Ryan, who ran a dance academy in the city. He had heard my voice and thought if I could also tap dance I might become a young entertainer he could add to the talented concert party he ran. The company, all amateurs, gave hundreds of shows every year in and around St. John's. We only received sixpence or a shilling for each performance, but more important it was my first taste of the sweet sound of applause."

"Remember," said Donald Brian in 1943, "there were no films, not even radio, at that time. Live concerts were the only form of public entertainment and people with nothing else to do packed the church halls and community halls every night of the week. I must have sung and danced to every Irish ballad ever written."

He told the *New York Times* in a feature story printed in 1928 that he had often wondered what happened to all the other singers, dancers and musicians who had appeared with him in those early days. "I recall many people who astonished me with their talents. Surely I was not the only one to reach success in New York City."

The story brought hundreds of letters to Donald Brian and the *New York Times*. Many were from former residents of St. John's then living in the United States. "Some were from people I remembered," he said. "I answered every letter, meeting in the years that followed many of the friends I had made when I was very much younger. I recalled their immense talents, but not one had, like me, found a way, or desire, to become a professional entertainer."

In 1943 Donald Brian said although George M. Cohan was always credited with discovering him and making him into a top-line entertainer, "It was Herbert O'Sullivan who developed my then soprano voice into the powerful, but well controlled tenor that has remained with me throughout my career, and it was Dennis Ryan who taught me many of the intricate dance steps that I was still using many years later. I am grateful to George M., but indebted forever to Mr. O'Sullivan and Mr. Ryan."

Donald Brian: The King of Broadway

Donald Brian remained in St. John's until 1893 when he was 18. At that time, he expected that the Newfoundland city would be his home for the rest of his life. But fate intervened, and when he and his mother left St. John's on July 4, 1893, their lives changed forever.

3 Heading to Boston

Returning home on July 1, 1893, after playing for the junior soccer team that represented St. John's, Donald Brian was surprised to find his mother in a serious conversation with Dennis Ryan, Herbert O'Sullivan and another lady he remembered as Molly O'Malley, a neighbour who had moved to Boston two years earlier.

Twenty years later, in 1913, Donald Brian recalled that day, and the days that followed, in detail for the *Green Book*, a magazine devoted to the New York theatre. The editor had invited twelve of the top Broadway stars to recall their most memorable Fourth of July.

"July the Fourth didn't mean as much to me then as it does today," wrote Donald Brian. "Everyone looked very solemn sitting around the parlour and I could see tears running down my mother's face. I was sure there had been some terrible tragedy, a tragedy that had brought them all together, a tragedy serious enough to make mother cry.

"Though everyone smiled as they looked at me, mother's tears didn't fit the moment so I rushed over to her to see what had happened. She assured me her tears were not caused by any tragedy and said Molly O'Malley, then Molly Reichert, had come to take us back with her to Boston.

"I protested. Why should we want to move to Boston? I felt we were doing fine in St. John's. I had graduated from high school in June and I would soon be working on one of the fishing trawlers bringing in extra money to the family. I told her that our good friends were all there. I didn't want to move away from St. John's.

"Molly Reichert explained that her husband Clive owned a large clothing production plant in Boston and she and her husband wanted mother to take over the plant as manager and designer. She said she had heard from friends how well mother was doing in the St. John's clothing factory and felt we could do much better for ourselves in Boston where I would have more opportunities to get a good job, helping bring financial security to the family.

"She even offered to find us a nice home in Boston, which we could pay for over ten years.

"Dennis Ryan obviously saw my dislike of the idea of leaving St. John's and told me there would be more chances for me as a singer and dancer in Boston.

"I told him I didn't want to leave St. John's. What would happen to the dancing act I did with Billy? Billy wouldn't be in Boston.

"Dennis helped me to accept the move. 'Perhaps Billy and I can come down to join you in a year or two,' he said 'All things are possible.'

"I didn't sleep that night. It just didn't make sense for us to leave our friends and the home we loved. But next morning mother told me she had agreed to go to Boston and that it would be the best thing for both of us if I agreed to make the move with her.

"Molly had asked that we make the journey immediately as her husband was overwhelmed with work and needed a plant manager immediately.

"Only three days later we had given away most of our furniture to people in need. Between us we packed five large suitcases and five wooden boxes that held special memories including more than twenty trophies I had won for my singing and dancing.

"On that memorable July the Fourth, Billy Ryan brought a Union Jack to the boat. It was the flag that showed Newfoundland's allegiance to England. I still have it and every July the Fourth I hang it outside my home alongside a larger United States Stars and Stripes.

"July 4, 1893 was the most important day in my life. Although I didn't know it then it was to lead me to success that I could never have hoped to achieve at home.

"Billy and I had waved until we could no longer see each other, then I stood at the stern of the ship until the last sight of land had vanished before going to my cabin where I cried myself to sleep.

"When later I understood what July the Fourth meant to every American, I used that day as one on which I would not go to bed unless I had done something to help someone, somewhere, as Molly Reichert had done for us on July 4, 1893.

"July the Fourth was, and always will be, the most important day of my life."

Donald Brian's life is full of July the Fourths on which he kept that promise. It is a life story in which he achieved great things and became a wealthy man. But, as his daughter Denise said in 2001, "He always gave back to the world much, much more than he ever received."

4 A Welcome from Boston

Clive Reichert arranged a never-to-be-forgotten welcome for Margaret and Donald Brian when the trawler carrying them, and his wife Molly, to Boston, arrived at the dock. He had hired a small brass band playing Irish tunes to greet them.

"I was stunned," Donald Brian told the *Boston Globe* in 1908. "He had his own horse and carriage waiting to pick up Molly, and beside it was another one to take mother and I to the new house in which we were to live. A horse-driven dray, containing all our luggage, arrived at the house less than an hour later.

"I remember everything in the cases and boxes smelled of fish. Mother washed all our clothes twice before I felt comfortable going out of the house to meet people. But within a week every trace of the odour had vanished.

"The house, a semi-detached stone bungalow, was much larger than our St. John's home. Mother and I were amazed to find it was completely furnished in beautiful style and from that moment we knew we were going to love America."

Clive Reichert's job offer to Margaret Brian turned out to be the dream job she had always hoped to find. Reichert paid top salaries to his employees and had one of the first private medical plans in the United States covering every worker and his or her family.

"It was a wonderful place to work," recalled Margaret Brian in her 1922 interview with the *New York Times*. "Clive was considerate to everyone. Although I left him sixteen years later to move here to New York where my son was, by then, a big star, we kept in touch until Clive and Molly were killed in a shocking accident in 1912 when a boulder crashed down from a cliff and crushed their automobile.

"Clive and Molly's two children, Patty and Henry, both came to New York and stayed in my home until they were settled. With Donny's help, Henry obtained an electrician's job in the theatre and soon became a very competent theatre lighting expert. Over the years he worked with great success, designing lighting for five of Donny's musicals.

"Patty trained at a New York theatre school to become an actress but, on a visit home to Boston, she met a man with whom she had attended high school. They were married two years later and are now living happily in California. Henry moved there too, going into the film industry when lighting became important. He is still there and is very successful. He works for Louis B. Mayer and has won several awards for his unique lighting systems."

Donald Brian's first job in Boston was in Clive Reichert's downtown clothing store, selling suits from the factory in which his mother worked.

"I think it was that job that taught him to dress immaculately, his trademark over the years, and when he was only twenty, he used to stand outside the doors of the store greeting everybody who passed by," Margaret Brian told the *New York Times*. "As he spoke he added a few clever dance steps and often crowds gathered to watch. Clive told me his personality, appearance and warm and honest smile doubled the sales of the store in less than six months. By the time he was twenty-one, he was managing the store. But he spent more time outside in front of the store than inside his office.

"In the middle of winter Donny kept a kettle boiling on a stove he installed just inside the doors and invited people to come inside for a cup of coffee or tea to keep warm.

"This was so very successful that when the small shop next door became vacant Donny and I rented it as a tea shop. With Clive's approval we had a hole cut in the wall between the two stores and customers at one store could walk, without going outside, into the other store. Both were great successes, especially in the winter months."

5 George M. Cohan

George M. Cohan remembered, in his first autobiography, the time he spotted Donald Brian on the sidewalk outside the store he managed.

"I had just left the theatre where I and my family, the Four Cohans, were rehearsing for our new show, when I heard these distinct fast-paced taps coming from across the street.

"I watched for a few moments and saw people had gathered around the dancer. I crossed the road and spoke to this immaculately dressed young man who I later learned was just twenty-one.

'Are you a professional dancer?' I asked.

'No,' said the young man.

'Then how would you like to join the Four Cohans road show company?' I said. At that moment a lady walked out of the front door of a small tea room next door.

'Get away you,' she said to me. 'I've heard all about your kind.'

"She chided her son not to talk to strangers, grabbed him by the ear and pulled him away.

"By this time a large crowd had gathered," said Cohan. "Many recognized me and started applauding. Obviously the lady who appeared to be the boy's mother did not know who I was.

'Madam,' I said, "'I'm George M. Cohan, principal dancer of the Four Cohans musical act, and, if you'll let me, I will make your son very famous on the Broadway stage.'

Margaret Brian suddenly realised to whom she was talking, and, said Cohan, "Blushed beet red."

George M. Cohan

Cohan took Brian and his mother back to the Boston theatre and two nights later Donald Brian made his debut as a professional entertainer.

Margaret Brian said that in 1912, it wasn't quite as easy as it sounds.

"I told Mr. Cohan that Donny would need a written contract and that my friend, Clive Reichert, would have to approve it before Donny signed.

"Later that afternoon, we all sat down in the office of a lawyer Clive had recommended, and later that same day, Donny signed his first professional contract. He won't mind me telling you now that his salary on the company's road tour was $10 a week, increasing to $15 when the show reached Broadway. Mr. Cohan assured me that Donny could get a clean room in which to live in one of the many theatrical boarding houses in every city that provided three meals a day for $5 a week. I laugh now when I think of those spotless rooms, including good Catholic meals with fish every Friday, that cost Donny only $4 or $5 a week."

Unhappily, the show was not one of the Cohan family's major successes and never did reach Broadway or New York.

"The forty-seven weeks I toured with the Cohans in the show gave me the confidence and the abilities that did take me to Broadway three years later in 1899," Donald Brian said in 1943.

"The Cohans treated me with utter kindness as they did to everyone else in the company. George M. Cohan was the unquestioned star of the family and his name was larger on the theatre posters than that of the family act, the Four Cohans. He spent hours with me enhancing the basic skills I had learned in St. John's.

"I remember one morning in Chicago, where we played for two weeks to packed houses, he walked onstage where I practised my dance steps every day. He watched quietly before walking over to me. 'Donald,' he said, 'I would like you to teach me the steps you have just been doing. I've never seen anything like those before, where did you learn them?'

'In St. John's, Newfoundland, my home,' I said. 'Dennis Ryan used them all the time and I just copied him.'

'Then the man must be a genius,' said Cohan. 'Those are unique steps, I must learn them.'

"Me, teaching George M. Cohan how to dance! I blushed deep red and said I couldn't possibly teach him anything.

'Never say that again to anyone,' said George M. 'One day, when you are a big star, and make no mistake you are going to be a big star, never refuse to help any dancer who hopes to equal your immense abilities. Now, teach me the steps.'

"I was actually shaking as I taught him the moves Dennis Ryan had taught me in St. John's. He slapped me on the back and said, 'When I've got the steps perfected, I'll let you know and we'll add them to one of the numbers we do together, but don't you dare use them until I have reached your level of competence.'

"I walked out of the theatre that morning floating on cloud nine. Me, as good as George M. Cohan? It didn't seem possible, but George M. Cohan himself had said it was possible.

"I continued to rehearse every morning, often spotting George M. sitting quietly in the darkened theatre watching. But he never again interrupted my practise."

In St. Louis, the next stop after Chicago, Donald Brian received another, very pleasant, shock. "As I reached the theatre from the train station I was astonished to see my name on the huge posters. It wasn't big, but it was there. It read, 'And introducing Broadway's next star, tap-dancer supreme, Donald Brian.'

"It was at that moment, for the first time, I began to believe George M. Cohan knew what he was talking about."

6 Broadway Bound

Over the next two years, Donald Brian worked in touring revues and in vaudeville theatres where he performed his own song and dance routine. For two months, when theatre work was sparse, he worked with one of the "medicine shows" that were all the rage in a world when any "doctor" could sell pills that did everything except, as Donald Brian said, "teach you how to dance."

"I simply stood in the crowd while 'Dr.' Homer G. Cornell sold a cure-all medicine called Shalmugra from the back step of a horse-drawn caravan.

"He called it a wonder drug," he said, laughing, in 1943. "It was 'guaranteed' to cure anything from gout to toothache. It would put a shine on shoes and keep insects out of a house if spread around the porch and each window. Its amazing properties varied from day to day as 'Dr.' Cornell thought of new cures, or heard of a widespread problem in whichever town we visited. It sold for one dollar a bottle and it was my job to buy the first bottle each day to get the customers interested. Then I had to buy extra bottles and convince all the other buyers that they would need several bottles to gain all the benefits the elixir offered. At most stops in small town market squares he would sell more than 200 bottles. At night I had to boil up more supplies over an open fire beside the caravan. What I was boiling I never did find out, but the smell at times was so bad I was grateful when we had everything corked in the bottles that filled about half the caravan.

"The 'doctor' also sold a liniment made of naphtha and red pepper. This one was 'guaranteed' to cure, among other things, a man or woman of deafness in twenty-four hours or remove warts or blemishes from the face or hands in less than forty-eight hours. A small metal container of the lotion cost fifty cents, and we sold thousands in the eight weeks I was with him. I got a dollar a day, all my food, which he cooked over an open fire, and a bunk in the caravan in which we lived. The horse ate the same food as us; more often than not its meal was whatever I had left over as being unpalatable.

"Whether the medicine or liniment was any good I never did find out. Long before the customers had tried the medicine and might possibly be seeking a refund, we had left town and were miles away.

"You will read stories that I appeared in several plays at that period in my career including *The New Boy* and *The Chaperones*, and that I made my New York debut in something called *Three Little Lambs* at the Fifth Avenue Theatre. Someone created those stories and other writers just picked them up as being true. But I had never heard of the three plays until I read in newspaper stories that I had appeared in them."

At that period in his career the nearest Donald Brian came to Broadway was when he got his first booking in one of New York's many luxurious nightclubs.

He had kept in touch with George M. Cohan and one night in the fall of 1899 the great entertainer, then working as a solo performer, starring in New York and in the biggest theatres across the United States, came to see Donald at the club where he was working.

'Donny,' said Cohan, 'a friend of mine is about to start rehearsals for a Broadway musical he has called *On the Wabash*. He has asked me to invite you to be part of that show. In addition to one or two solo spots you will help the choreographer with all the dance routines in the show. I have negotiated a contract that will pay you $35 a week plus an advance cash payment of $100 for your assistance with the choreography.

'If that is acceptable we must meet in the morning at the theatre to sign the contract. Although you are now twenty-four and of course do not need your mother's approval, I must tell you I have already been in touch with her in Boston and she has given her blessing to the terms of the contract. She was thrilled that you were soon to be on Broadway. Now what do you say?'

Broadway Bound

"What did I say," recalled Brian in 1907 to the *New York World* when overnight he had become the most important name on Broadway. "I said, 'Thank you, thank you, Mr. Cohan. I'll never forget you. One day perhaps I can do something for you.'

'Right now' said Cohen, 'you can do something very important for me. You will soon be on Broadway so it is time you stopped calling me Mr. Cohan. I'd like it if you called me George M.'

"Once he had left I remember waltzing around the dressing room at the club singing, I can call him George M. George M. George M."

When Donald Brian started being offered regular New York nightclub work, he moved into a furnished two-room apartment on 47th Street, just off Broadway. He paid four dollars a week in rent. It had a small kitchen in which he made all his own meals.

Perhaps looking forward to the day when the opportunity George M. had just put in his lap would come along, he attended, when permitted by the choreographers in charge, rehearsals of many of the Broadway musicals in preparation.

"Looking back now," he said in 1943, "I have to wonder why so many choreographers allowed me to help, free of charge, but not one offered me a job.

"But I soon became well known to many of the young New York chorus girls who I tried to help, if they were struggling with particularly difficult steps. Tap dancing was the big thing then in theatres staging musicals, and in vaudeville, and as George M. had once told me, I had a few tap steps that were unique.

"Although I wasn't supposed to take in extra residents in my apartment, it became known that any chorus girl out of work could knock on my door and find a bed in which to sleep and sufficient food to allow her to eat regular meals until work came along. It was a benefit to me too. I got all my meals prepared and put on the table at regular hours. Many of the girls I was able to introduce to nightclub managements and almost all got work quickly."

Donald Brian: The King of Broadway

On the Wabash was not a major success, running for only twenty-seven performances, but it resulted in dozens of offers for Donald Brian.

It also brought a special visitor to a matinee performance of *On the Wabash*. On a day that her own musical did not have an afternoon show, Lillian Russell, then known as the "Queen of Broadway" and acclaimed as one of the most beautiful women in the world, visited Brian in his dressing room after his show.

Twenty-six years later, long after they were married, Donald Brian told his new wife the story of their conversation. Virginia kept the secret until 1949, a few months after Donald Brian's death, before telling the *New York Times* the bizarre story of Lillian Russell's visit.

"Miss Russell, no longer alive, will surely not mind now having the story of that meeting told," she said. "She didn't knock, walking right into Donny's dressing room while he was changing into his street clothes.

"She said, 'I see, Mr. Brian, that you hide your greatest assets from theatregoers, and although I will never appear with you since I fear I could not match your magical charm onstage, I would like to give you the opportunity of sharing my bed in my New York home tonight so we can decide once and for all who is the greatest performer.'

"Donny bowed, wrapping a towel around his exposed body, and asked Miss Russell to sit down.

'Your offer is not one that I dismiss lightly,' he said, 'and one which I am sure few other men in New York would turn down, but I must refuse. As a Catholic, I promised the church when I was sixteen that my first bedding would be with the woman I chose to be my wife.'

'Then make this offer also my proposal of marriage to you, Mr. Brian,' said Miss Russell who had just been divorced from her third husband.

'With sadness and regret I reject that proposal too,' said Brian. 'I know your reputation as an incomparable artiste, but as a woman with whom I would wish to spend my entire life, I know insufficient.'

"Lillian Russell rose, bowed to Donny, and said, 'Goodnight Mr. Brian. If you change your mind let me know.' She left the room with what Donny recalled was the most seductive smile he had ever seen."

The next day, Lillian Russell spoke to a reporter from the *New York World*. She had this to say about the Newfoundland-born star's performance:

> "I attended the matinee of *On the Wabash* yesterday to see if I might, in the future, team up with this remarkable young man, Donald Brian, who is receiving such amazing reviews in a show that I now know is unworthy of his talents. It took me less than thirty minutes to realise that a teaming of he and I would be totally impossible.
>
> "I like to be the unquestioned star, the greatest talent, in any show in which I appear, and if Mr. Brian and I worked together that would be an impossible task for me.
>
> "His every appearance onstage drew gasps from the large majority of young ladies in his audience and I felt sorry for the other artistes who were overwhelmed by his personality, charm, dignity, manner and outrageous dancing and singing talents. No, Mr. Brian and I will never appear together on a stage, much as I regret making that an irrevocable decision."

That decision was to be reconsidered in 1908, when Lillian Russell and Donald Brian agreed to a request from George M. Cohan to appear together at a Sunday charity concert. Her comment on that appearance stunned the audience with its audacity. But many more things happened to Donald Brian before that incident, which was talked about for many years in New York theatre circles.

Before *On the Wabash* closed, Sydney Rosenfeld, who had written a new musical scheduled to open in a few months at the Winter Garden Theatre in New York, approached him on the street after the evening show.

"Mr. Brian," he said, "If you could spare the time tomorrow, I would like to introduce you to Donald Sime who, with his brother Alex, will stage my new show, *The Supper Club*, in January of next year. Donald and Alex have seen your performance in *On the Wabash* and suggested I see the show. I did that tonight, and address you now in the hope that you might agree to be the lead performer in my show."

Donald Brian requested that Rosenfeld have the show music ready to play for him in the Sime brothers' office the following morning. "I'll be delighted to consider your proposal," he said, "but must first read the script and hear the music."

Two days later, the New York *Daily World* printed a story that Donald Brian had signed to star in *The Supper Club* show scheduled to open in January.

"I asked for and received forty dollars a week to be increased to fifty dollars if the show exceeded twenty performances. In those days a show that lasted forty nights was classed as a hit," he said.

The Supper Club, more of a revue than a musical, featured Donald Brian as dancer and singer and, for the first time, gave him billing in the program as the choreographer.

"I emptied my apartment of out-of-work dancers, getting all eight into the show," he recalled. The show was also the Broadway debut of Al Hart, a young comedian from Toronto, Canada, who later went on to considerable fame in the New York theatre and as a talented mime in early silent films in California."

Official records of Broadway shows in which Donald Brian was said to have appeared include the suggestion that he starred at the same Winter Garden Theatre only days after *The Supper Club* closed in a revival of an earlier Broadway musical success, *Floradora*.

Broadway Bound

In 1943, looking through his large collection of programs from Broadway shows he produced one from *Floradora*. "See for yourself," he said. "I am not listed in the program and never appeared in the show. I can only presume now, after all these years, that the Sime brothers hoped to cash in on my *Supper Club* success by adding my name to every press release they sent out about *Floradora*, but I never at any time agreed to be part of the show.

"*Floradora* was not an original show, but a revival of a production that ran for more than eighty performances in 1898. The revival was not a success and on the night I saw the show as a member of the audience I got, if you'll forgive my boasting, more applause on my arrival than did the company at the final curtain."

In 1901, with no new stage show in the offing, Donald Brian was more than a little surprised to receive an invitation to try out for a place on the Brooklyn Superbas, the most talked about young baseball team in the area.

"I had first learned about baseball in Boston and was soon playing for the best team in the city. I had played cricket in St. John's, Newfoundland, but this much more intricate game of hitting a round ball on a round bat quickly knocked all thoughts of cricket out of my mind. It turned out that one of the Superbas, Harry Lumley, who had been in the Boston team where I played, saw *The Supper Club* and remembered me, not as a performer, but as a baseball player who could hit.

"I went down to their ground and had my tryout. But they offered me only ten dollars a week so I turned down their invitation to become a professional baseball player.

"But I did attend all their games. They were always held in afternoons because lighting for night games didn't exist at that time. I got into many of the games somewhat illegally as I was never officially on the club roster and now and then someone slipped a five-dollar bill in my hand if we won.

"I never became a regular player and in January 1902, the Sime brothers approached me again to appear at the Winter Garden Theatre in a new musical, *The Belle of Broadway*.

Donald Brian: The King of Broadway

"It wasn't a major production with a cast of only seventeen, but the music was good, the dialogue above average and with eight of my chorus girls onstage it was a pleasant time for the six weeks it survived."

Donald Brian then went back into the city's nightclubs, commanding a salary of $100 to $200 a week.

"In many cases I did a one-man show with a five-piece band, so they saved money by not having to hire any supporting acts. This was the first time I had done one-man comedy in addition to my dancing and singing, but it was very successful and soon I had more job offers than I could handle."

George M. Cohan came back into his life in 1904 with an offer to appear in the new musical show he had written, *Little Johnny Jones*.

"I'd like you to join me for this show," he said to Donald Brian. "I will give you equal billing with myself. Your salary will be seventy dollars a week and a percentage of the money we take at the box-office each week."

"That was the first occasion I realised how valuable a percentage of the weekly ticket sales could be," said Brian. "We ran for ten very successful weeks and in addition to my salary I received more than $3,000 from my share of the profits."

In the cast with George M. and Donald Brian were two other members of the once renowned Four Cohans, his mother, Helen, and his father, Jerry. His sister, Josephine, had left the act when she married a wealthy New York banker. *Little Johnny Jones* was to be the final appearance for both Helen and Jerry. They too were scheduled to retire when the show closed.

"George M. was a wealthy man and I know from seeing the beautiful home he built for his parents that he kept them in luxury for the rest of their lives," Donald said in 1943. "He died last November 5, [1942], and I was one of the honorary pallbearers at his funeral. Thousands congregated outside the church unable to find a seat in the church. I saw Bing Crosby with tears streaming down his face standing in the crowd; he had not been able to get inside."

Broadway Bound

During his illustrious career, Cohan wrote more than fifty plays and musicals, and it was his proud boast that not one ever lost money for its backers.

After the successful New York run, Cohan wanted to take *Little Johnny Jones* on the road to twenty-eight different cities. His parents felt they were too old to tour and in his autobiography Cohan said if Donald Brian had not agreed to the tour it would never have got off the ground.

He asked Brian to sign a twenty-eight week contract. Cohan suggested he take no salary but a 25 percent share of the tour profits.

"By now I knew I could trust George M. with my life and I never did have a written contract for the tour. We just shook hands and I needed no accountant to tell me I was going to get every penny to which I was entitled.

"Although few people outside New York had heard about me, my name was on the billboards as big as that of George M. The successful tour was extended to forty weeks.

"I used my new knowledge about taking shares in a production to my benefit in the future. From that day onwards, I always asked for a lower salary and a percentage of the profits or the box-office take. One or two managements tried to hide the real income of the show, but when I realised this I asked for an added clause in all my contracts giving me the right to ask for an independent accountant to audit the show's weekly returns. I estimate my accountant saved me more than a quarter of a million dollars in the years from 1907 to 1933."

Cohan wrote this in his autobiography. "Although his first Broadway show, *On the Wabash* was unsuccessful he had proved himself to be a sterling performer with few equals. The tour of *Little Johnny Jones* was extended because managements in all parts of the country heard about his achievements onstage during the tour and for the first time in my career I was not receiving the greatest applause at the end of each night's performance."

Ethel Levey, a major Broadway star, who had played in New York in *Little Johnny Jones*, had also agreed to the tour. To ensure he could keep her in the show George M. Cohan married her.

In 1908 she spoke to the *Green Room* magazine. "I do not believe I have ever worked with a more amiable, down to earth genius than I did in the *Little Johnny Jones* show with Donald Brian. His stature increased with every performance and keeping up with his talent was so impossible that I threw up my hands and allowed him to be the unquestioned star of the show.

"My husband at that time, George M. Cohan, told me that playing second fiddle to this genius would bring in the crowds to the box-office. If we had an empty seat in any theatre during the forty-week tour I didn't see it. We all made a lot of money.

"Donny had made a special request to George M. before he would agree to do the tour. He made George M. sign contracts with all the dancers guaranteeing them fifteen dollars a week, more than three times the four dollars they got on Broadway.

"I always remember his generosity to the young dancers in the show. Morning after morning he would be onstage with them helping increase their knowledge of dancing and stage movement. Those young ladies worshipped Donny. They waited outside his hotel every morning so they could walk to the theatre with him.

"One of the girls, Rosemary Grosz, told me they loved him because he never once made an improper advance to any of them. Rosemary went with him in a featured role in his next appearance for George M., but went back in the chorus line so she could be with him in the big show that finally made Donny a star.

"She told me they once feared Donny was a poof [homosexual] but they watched him working with the men in the company and soon realised he was just a wonderful man and very definitely not a poof.

"Rosemary said she would have married him in a minute but he never asked! He told me one day that when the right girl came along he would waste no time getting married.

Broadway Bound

"I was a veteran Broadway artiste by that time but I often stood offstage watching, more often than not picking up gems of his immense knowledge of dancing and stage craft that he was never afraid to share with others.

"I remember about four weeks out of New York seeing George M. watching Donny Brian work with his mouth wide open in wonder."

"His day will come in New York," said George M., "and when it does arrive it will be a day never to be forgotten on Broadway."

He was right! But that day was still three years away.

Donald Brian was never again out of work. "I worked only in the most exclusive nightclubs and was earning as much as $250 a week. By 1905 I had bought a beautiful six-room penthouse apartment on 51st Street, furnishing it myself. It was unique since I was the only tenant of the suite named on the lobby residents' board, but it boasted ten extra beds in addition to my own. The era was not a good one for Broadway dancers and I often had as many as ten young dancers living and eating there with me."

That same year George M. Cohan came back into his life.

'I have written and am about to produce a new musical revue, *Forty-five Minutes from Broadway*,' he said. 'I want you to be the star of the show. Fay Templeton [a star in her own right in that era] will be with you and I want you to help me get the finest performers that money can buy for even the smallest roles. How does that sound? I promised your mother I would make you into a Broadway star. That time has arrived. You will walk away after the show closes with a star hung around your neck.'

"I am rarely short of words," said Donald Brian in 1907 to the *New York World*, "but I was stunned to silence by George M's generosity and prediction.

"When I recovered I came down to earth long enough to ask George M. if he would agree to audition the six girls then living in my apartment for the chorus.

"He hired every one of them, and gave Rosemary Grosz her first speaking role in the show. Six more I suggested he hired to complete the chorus without even auditioning them, guaranteeing them contracts that almost doubled the pay that most dancers received on Broadway at that time. He had only one stipulation before agreeing. I had to create the dance routines for the show. He even gave me $500 up front for the choreography. My weekly salary on the road for six weeks was to be $100 and on Broadway $150 a week. Add to this the percentage of the box-office take I was to receive, and that was very big money in those days.

"I also suggested to him that one of the musical numbers that had received so much applause in *Little Johnny Jones* be used again in the new show. I pointed out that the song was still being whistled and sung around New York, and probably in every city we had visited on the tour too.

"He wasn't too thrilled with the idea but finally agreed to find a place for *Give My Regards to Broadway* in the new show and night after night it stopped the show."

In his autobiography George M. Cohan wrote: "That was the one and only time I repeated a song in any of the fifty shows I wrote and produced. But it was a good suggestion from Donny. I was quickly beginning to realise he understood audiences better than anyone, including myself."

Forty-five Minutes from Broadway gave Donald Brian his first look at the beautiful New Amsterdam Theatre on 42nd Street. He little realised at that time that only a year later he would be called the biggest star on Broadway while appearing in the same theatre in a spectacular new production.

Forty-five Minutes from Broadway opened the first of its three out-of-town tryout weeks in Boston.

"On the opening night mother sat with Molly and Clive in the best stage box in the house. The friends I had made while I worked in the clothing store all attended and much to my embarrassment they gave me a standing ovation when I walked onstage for the first time. That was before I had even spoken or sung a word or danced a step.

I was told later that Clive Reichert had bought 300 tickets for his employees and their families.

"When we opened on Broadway my name, for the first time, was the only name above the title of the show.

"We had been running only a few days when I was called to go immediately after the show into George M.'s stage-side office. I was receiving a lot of applause each night and couldn't imagine what I had done to receive such an urgent summons. I hoped I had not offended the gracious Fay Templeton who seemed to have accepted without any question having her name lower down on the posters than mine. Before *Forty-five Minutes*, she had been the top star in a number of very successful Broadway shows.

"When I knocked on George M.'s office door he opened it with a big smile. Perhaps the news was to be good.

"A man sitting in the corner of the room rose to his feet and put his hand out for me to shake. I was almost too stunned to say anything. George M.'s guest was the President of the United States, Theodore Roosevelt.

'I was in the audience tonight and must say you are an amazing performer,' said the president. 'I have told Mr. Cohan that I will bet him $500 that you will be the most important star on Broadway within three years. We have a deal, have we not, Mr. Cohan?'

"Cohan raised his hands in despair. 'This is a gamble I don't like to take because I know I am certain to lose, Mr. President, but you are the most important man in our nation so I must, with reluctance, accept your bet. Donald Brian is one of the most impressive performers I have ever been associated with throughout my career.'

Two days later, Donald Brian discovered that George M. Cohan was never one to miss any opportunity for publicity. "Beneath my name," he said, "pasted on every billboard in the city he had added one extra line: 'Soon to become Broadway's greatest star,' says President Theodore Roosevelt."

Three days later President Roosevelt returned to see the show for a second time. "This time, after the show, he headed not for George M.'s stage-side office, but my dressing room," recalled Brian in a *New York Times* interview in 1932. "He greeted me as though I was an important man. 'Sir, would you dine with me this evening?' he asked. In those days no performer ate before a strenuous show so I accepted with pleasure. I did suggest that we might take George M. along with us, but he dismissed the idea, adding, 'My friend, it is you to whom I wish to talk.'

During his lifetime Donald Brian never revealed details of the conversation he had with President Roosevelt that evening. On many occasions he refused to answer the question from writers. "My conversation with President Roosevelt was a private matter," he would say. "One doesn't discuss details of private conversations with the president of the United States."

Just after Donald Brian's death in 1948, his widow said this to the *New York Times*. "President Roosevelt asked if my husband would teach him how to relax in public. He told Donny that although he had been president for four years he still tightened up whenever he was called upon to speak and wanted to know how Donny was so totally at ease and relaxed in every situation.

'I would like to enjoy the friendliness from my audiences that you evoke from yours,' he said.

"Donny told him being relaxed just came to him naturally, but he spent many afternoons with the president over the next two weeks and told him a secret he had never told anyone else.

"He said he always concentrated on just one person in his audience, a person who looked happy to be there, and he directed his entire performance to that one individual.

"Several months later, President Roosevelt sent him a letter thanking him for his advice, saying how much more comfortable he now felt in front of an audience.

"I am the only person who ever saw that letter. Donny felt it would be improper to suggest a President of the United States needed help from an entertainer.

"The president added that using Donny's advice he had been able to lower the tone of his previously rather high pitched voice considerably.

"But we have both agreed the letter will one day be given to our daughter, Denise."

In 2001, Denise confirmed that she had the letter, but had always refused to show it to anyone. "My father would never allow anyone to see it and to break his confidence, and the confidence of President Theodore Roosevelt, would be wrong, very wrong," she said.

7 Almost Stardom

Forty-five Minutes from Broadway **was the biggest hit of the 1906 New York** theatre season. *Give My Regards to Broadway* was played, whistled and sung everywhere in the city. Every music store in town ran out of piano copies of the music and George M. Cohan said in 1942, to the *New York Daily News*, that the music publisher ordered an immediate second printing of 20,000 more copies with Donald Brian's picture on the front cover.

"I get only a few cents royalty from every sheet of music sold," he said, "but I have made a lot of money from that song alone. It still sells today and at a guess I would say it has made me in excess of $200,000," he said. "I was told recently it sold more than two million copies."

Donald Brian recalled that on many occasions when he entered public restaurants with friends, the diners would rise to their feet applauding and singing the superb Cohan song. "I had to stand wherever I was until they had finished singing then, and only then, would the maitre'd show me and my friends to our table and I was applauded every step of the way. I always added a few intricate dance steps en route to our table and the diners yelled with delight. It was an exciting time in my life.

"Every good restaurant of that era boasted a piano-player, some even an orchestra, and astute managers alerted them to the reservations I made. I learned many months later that a flashlight was placed at the entrance to the restaurants I patronized regularly and when I arrived it was flashed three times to tell the pianist or bandleader I was there. A piano fanfare or a blare of trumpets let other diners know I had entered the restaurant.

"The only good thing that came out of those occasions was that nine times out of ten the manager refused to give me a bill saying, 'The meals are on the house.'"

Another song from the show, *Mary is a Grand Old Name*, was almost as well received and George M. Cohan decided to be generous and offer every seat in the house at half-price at a special matinee performance to persons who could provide written proof that their names were Mary. The extra matinee performance was added with all the proceeds going to a fund to help out-of-work entertainers, and Cohan reports in his autobiography that "Every seat was sold out in five days. We let the papers know that Marie's and other variations of Mary would also be admitted half price. That day we had 1,600 Marys or variations including Marigolds, yelling for Donny for nearly three hours. Their husbands and boyfriends had to wait for them outside. The only man in the house that matinee was a man who proved, by his birth certificate, that his name was Marie Sellinger. He explained that his mother had wanted a daughter and she was so mad when he came along that she christened him Marie.

"We gathered so much press space from this one show it would have filled a complete scrapbook. There were few photographs in the papers in those days, but a picture of Marie Sellinger standing with Donny and the prettiest of the Marys present made the front page of the *New York Post*."

The musical's title song, *Forty-five Minutes from Broadway*, was the show's third hit. There were reports, said Cohan in his memoirs, that club singers who couldn't or wouldn't sing the three songs were booed off the club stages.

George M. Cohan said, "I thank heaven Donny never wanted to be a writer of shows or music so I was able to hold my head above water for many years in that respect after he became an enormous star in his own right."

Forty-Five Minutes from Broadway ran for forty-seven weeks, a major success for a Broadway show of that era. Donald Brian never missed a performance and often joined George M. Cohan who volunteered their services, during the run of the musical, at more than thirty benefit shows held on Sundays to raise money for different needy charities.

"Those performances were duels between Donny and I," said Cohan in a *New York Post* story in 1914, "We always did separate acts before singing and dancing together [in] *Give My Regards to Broadway*. We took our musical director, Louis Gottschalk, from the theatre to conduct our acts and when the audiences kept on applauding for our duet and dancing as they always did, Lou knew just how long to keep the music going, chorus after chorus. I used to scratch my left ear when we wanted Lou to end the number.

"I remember one Sunday when we were appearing in a benefit for the New York chorus boys and girls we had to keep dancing and singing for eighteen choruses until I signalled to Lou that we were exhausted. Even when the music stopped they were still shouting for more and Donny tapped and I sang one more chorus before running, perhaps staggering would be a more truthful word, offstage.

"Sitting in the wings of the theatre was a wheelchair later to be used in a scene from a play, so I told Donny to sit in the chair and I wheeled him across to the other side. The exhaustion that showed on my face was not make-believe, and the audience rose to its feet as one."

During the run of *Forty-five Minutes from Broadway*, Donald Brian was introduced to silent film director Sidney Olcott, then working at the Kalem Film Company studio in New York City.

"I had learned of Sid Olcott's successes in the quickly growing silent movie industry, so I asked if I might visit the studio to see the making of a film," he said in 1943.

"I was astonished, after the luxury of most Broadway theatres, to discover his studio was little more than a large empty room in which they built half a dozen or more primitive sets. Since there was no sound, many sets were almost side by side and on my first visit I watched a death scene in a small bedroom and a villain shooting silently at a different family on another set just feet away. I marvelled at the ability of the actors to concentrate with so many distractions and soon became totally enamoured with this new entertainment media.

"Before I knew it, I was playing roles in many different films and visiting the studio, where Sid Olcott worked, almost every day. I recall playing six different roles in one single day. Sid Olcott thanked me for saving them from having to pay other actors for the work. I have often chided Sid with the fact that he never offered me a cent for my work.

"At that time in the film industry, none of New York's top theatre actors would agree to work in the film studios, as they believed the industry was nothing more than a fad which would soon die out. Being seen in the simple and often crudely made films, they believed, would destroy their hard-earned stage reputations.

"They didn't name their actors in those days and at no time was I ever credited on the screen for my roles. But it was fun, and Sid Olcott was undoubtedly one of the brightest lights in the world of silent films. He was a brilliant director who I tried, and failed, to lure into live theatre directing.

"If I had to guess, I must have played a hundred different roles between 1906 and 1910. The parts ranged from moustachioed villains to kindly ministers and now and then doddery old grandfathers. If I had a spare moment, I headed for the studio. And Sid told me that my contributions to the industry as an actor might never be remembered, but my knowledge of theatre had enabled me to show him how to get better use of simple lighting to get clearer pictures than ever before, eliminating the frustrating shadows that often marred the films of that early era.

"I even convinced him to build a house set much larger than usual on the flat roof of the studio where he could use natural daylight for lighting. Using the big set provided continuity as the characters moved from one room to the other without the sudden break from scene to scene that was traditional then in the small studios.

"I loved the film industry, but the theatre was far superior financially."

8 Unexpected Visitor

In January of 1907, Donald Brian received an unexpected visitor who would change his life forever.

"Our stage director approached me before the show to ask if I would be willing to meet after the show with a composer called Franz Lehar," he recalled in 1943. "He said Mr. Lehar was visiting the United States from Vienna to discuss the production in New York of a new operetta for which he had written the music. It had already been a big success in his native Austria.

"With him were the two libretto writers, Victor Leon and Leo Stein. None of them spoke much English so they were travelling with an interpreter. Mr. Lehar had asked if I would be willing to listen to some of the music from the show so I agreed to meet them in the theatre green room where there was a piano.

"I shook hands with all the visitors and the interpreter and requested that Mr. Lehar play one or two of the tunes he had written. An hour later I was still listening and applauding each remarkable melody.

'What is this operetta to be called,' I asked the interpreter.

'In German it is *Die Lustige Witwe*, but if you will accept a rough translation,' he said, 'I think it will be *The Merry Widow*'

'Will you play the lead role of Prince Danilo? And, if you are still with *Forty-five Minutes from Broadway* next year we will wait for you,' said Lehar partly in halting English, partly through his interpreter.

"We were in our second year with *Forty-five Minutes* and I told him I was under contract to Mr. Cohan for the run of the show.

"I advised him I expected the musical would run for several more months, but believed I might be able to appear in his musical in the fall of 1907. 'Could you accept that date?' I asked.

"Mr. Lehar rose from the piano stool and embraced me. With his few English words he said, 'Mr. Brian, we wait to eternity for you. Our operetta would not be complete without you as its star. With you as its star it will be unforgettable.'

"I was already in love with the enchanting music and knew I must play Prince Danilo. That it had been offered to me before any other performer seemed like a miracle.

"The next night, President Roosevelt came to see *Forty-five Minutes* again and once more we dined together. I had memorized much of the haunting music and sang the lilting waltz songs to him with la-la-la in place of the words that had not yet been written in English.

"It was President Theodore Roosevelt who gave the show's most memorable song its unofficial name, *The Merry Widow Waltz*. The glorious waltz number was so beautiful I couldn't get it out of my mind.

'I shall be there on your first night sitting in a box with George M. and after the show I shall collect the $500 from Mr. Cohan in your presence.' said President Roosevelt. 'On that night, Donald, you will become the biggest star on Broadway.'

Cohan told the *New York Post* in 1942, only a few months before his death, "I was not too happy to give a definite date for *Forty-five Minutes* to close its doors. It was drawing full houses every night and both Donny and I were making a lot of money.

"I had hoped to take the show on the road for perhaps fifty weeks, but when I heard the marvellous captivating music written by Mr. Lehar, I knew it would be impossible to keep Donny away from what I knew was to be the show that only comes once in a lifetime.

"In my entire career I have never competed for applause with a performer as talented as Donald Brian, but I have seen all his Broadway shows and we have remained the best of friends for more than forty years."

President Theodore Roosevelt was his pal. Donald Brian could walk nowhere in public without being stopped dozens of times by autograph collectors. People applauded whenever he entered a room. George M. Cohan had acknowledged him as an equal.

His mother was ready to make a move to New York to an apartment he had leased for her. He was still in touch with Billy Ryan who was serving in the British Navy. Sadly he had learned of the deaths of both Herbert O'Sullivan and Dennis Ryan.

"What have you left to accomplish?" he was asked by the *New York Post* on the closing night of *Forty-five Minutes from Broadway*.

"I have not yet found the lady I want to make my wife, a lady who will want to spend the rest of her days with me," he answered.

He was to wait twelve more years before the right woman finally came into his life, but it was six years after that before he plucked up the courage to ask her to marry him. When she did say "yes," they remained happily married, as he had always hoped, for the rest of their lives.

In 1943 Donald Brian said he never anticipated the success and admiration that was waiting around the corner in 1907.

"Nobody in his right mind could have visualised the events that unfolded that year," he said. "After the opening of *The Merry Widow* I realised that I was perhaps the luckiest person on earth. I spent the rest of my life trying to convince people down on their luck to keep dreaming because I had discovered that dreams really could come true."

9 The Merry Widow

The opening night of Herbert W. Savage's production of *The Merry Widow* was scheduled for Monday, October 21, 1907, at the New Amsterdam Theatre on 42nd Street. Somehow, George M. Cohan had convinced Donald Brian, with the approval of Herbert Savage, to extend the run of *Forty-five Minutes from Broadway* until October 2, less than three weeks before the opening of the new show, and only five days before its out-of-town tryout in New Haven, Connecticut.

In 1943 Donald Brian recalled wondering if he had made a mistake in agreeing to the extra two weeks.

"Rehearsing all day and performing at night was a major undertaking, but Ethel Jackson, who had been chosen from the hundreds of dancers and singers Herbert Savage and I auditioned to play Sonia, the Merry Widow, was a real trouper and she agreed that she and I would rehearse together every morning from the middle of September.

"We met at nine each day at a rehearsal studio on 44th Street. Franz Lehar himself played the piano for all the morning rehearsals. We chose this particular studio because its newly laid, very smooth, floor was absolutely perfect for trying out the intricate and unique dance steps we planned to unveil to our audiences on October 21.

"We broke for a light lunch at one, then walked from the restaurant to the New Amsterdam Theatre to join the rest of the cast waiting there on the stage that had been cleared of the *Forty-five Minutes* scenery and sets to allow four more hours of *Merry Widow* rehearsals. By 5:00 p.m., Ethel and I were so exhausted that when we relaxed in the two comfortable chairs in my dressing room we usually fell asleep within minutes, leaving strict instructions to be awakened at 7:00 p.m.

"Ethel then rejoined *The Merry Widow* cast in the rehearsal room on 44th Street and most nights rehearsed there for several more hours. I changed into my opening costume for the first act of *Forty-five Minutes* and waited for the fifteen-minute bell to alert me to be onstage.

"Between 7:00 and 8:00 p.m., I read and re-read every line of the wonderful *Merry Widow* script. The dialogue was totally down-to-earth, it had meaning, something completely new in New York Theatre where most dialogue in musicals was intended to be very frothy and unrealistic."

In his autobiography, George M. Cohan remembered something that Donald Brian never mentioned. He said, "Donny was adored by everyone, especially the ladies, and busy as he was he would often go to the stage door half an hour before curtain time, with two security guards. There he would sign autographs for the hundreds of young ladies waiting to see him every night. He seemed inexhaustible and that never changed throughout his long career. He never tired and he never ignored even the youngest child seeking his autograph.

"I had created a monster, but a charming, talented, and very loveable monster."

"We both knew that when the glorious waltz, *I Love You So*, was heard by the public for the first time the waltz would never be the same again," said Donald Brian.

"President Roosevelt who had christened it *The Merry Widow Waltz* when I first la-la-ed the melody to him over supper months earlier, repeated the name on the show's opening night. He called loudly from his box for a *Merry Widow Waltz* encore, and the audience echoed and re-echoed his call and his name for the song, *The Merry Widow Waltz*, was its only name from then on. If you asked in a music store for the piano music for *I Love You So* they wouldn't know what you were talking about.

"Within days of the opening the official title, *I Love You So*, was completely forgotten as everyone whistled and sang what became known only as *The Merry Widow Waltz*.

"After the opening night, every copy of *I Love You So* was sold out in New York's many music stores within two days and when the music publisher had it reprinted its title was what President Roosevelt had suggested, simply *The Merry Widow Waltz*."

Two weeks before the official opening, *The Merry Widow* had its first complete run-through on the New Amsterdam Theatre stage. The theatre was supposed to be closed to everyone other than the cast and individuals connected to the production. Somehow a young reporter managed to slip through the theatre's security men and watched most of the show before being ejected after he unwisely revealed himself when he failed to stop applauding and cheering the performance.

The writer revealed many years later in a *New York Times* story how he managed to get through the security guards who were positioned at every entrance.

"There were a number of pieces of discarded scenery lying in the alley beside the theatre so I just picked up the largest I could find and walked to the scenery dock, smiled at the guard, saying something like 'Scene Six' and walked into the theatre. He never gave me a second glance. I dropped the scenery side stage where I thought it would not be in the way, and slipped through the door from side stage to the auditorium and sat down in the darkest corner I could find."

The paper's editor was so enthused at getting the scoop that he not only gave the reporter a by-line with his first published story, but added him to the *Times* staff as a cub reporter at seven dollars a week.

Alexander Woollcott, the writer, in later years became one of the paper's most renowned theatre critics. He wrote books and in his distinguished lifetime penned many successful plays, one of which won a Pulitzer Prize.

This is what Mr. Woollcott wrote about *The Merry Widow*:

> "On October 21 a brand new era in New York theatre will begin. *The Merry Widow*, due to open on that day at the New Amsterdam Theatre on 42nd Street will bring to the city some of the most glorious and awe-inspiring music ever heard on any stage.

Donald Brian: The King of Broadway

"It will open new doors with its exciting and realistic dialogue and its spectacular stage settings will make you believe you have moved on a cloud of joy to another world.

"But above all, it is the actor playing, singing and dancing the role of Prince Danilo who will remain in your hearts for all time. Mr. Donald Brian, who only recently ended two years in Mr. George M. Cohan's *Forty-five Minutes from Broadway*, has created a very stirring and poignant character of Prince Danilo that will never be forgotten. After tomorrow night Mr. Brian will never be forgotten. His performance is almost immortal.

"His magic has inspired a very talented company to heights they surely never believed until now to be attainable or even imaginable. Miss Ethel Jackson, who plays the very Merry Widow in a flawless manner, helps Mr. Brian create dance steps never seen before on any stage. She could not reach the standard created by his twinkling feet but was never hesitant to try.

"Mr. Brian's very presence onstage seems to raise the level of wonder that shone across the footlights to inconceivable heights for the entire evening.

"I saw Mr. Franz Lehar, the Viennese composer, whose music, majestic, sensuous and exquisite, contributes so much to this breath-taking production, sitting alone in the otherwise empty front row of the theatre with both arms raised in wonderment at the spectacle he saw appearing onstage before his eyes.

"This musical masterpiece may run forever and I will be in the front row on opening night. I plan to be first in line at the theatre box office in the morning to book my seat for what I firmly believe will be the most thrilling theatrical event of this or any Broadway season."

The Merry Widow

Alexander Woollcott kept his word. He was first in line the next day when the newspaper published its theatrical scoop. He had received permission from the *Times* editor to delay his arrival for work at the newspaper office until after 10:00 a.m. so he could be at the box-office when it opened at that hour. Only a few stragglers joined him, but by noon, after his story had been read, the line of theatregoers stretched four wide from the theatre, down 42nd Street, and more than a hundred yards along the sidewalks of Broadway.

With only daily papers to create an interest in anything considered newsworthy, people who read the dignified *New York Times* accepted the stories they printed as being fact without any question, as Donald Brian discovered that morning. A bad review could close a show down quickly. A good review, especially a scoop like the one the *Times* had provided, could create almost a stampede for tickets.

"Walking down from my apartment on 51st Street, I wondered what on earth was happening," said Donald Brian in 1943. "I had never seen crowds like this in the city before and hot dog vendors were doing a roaring trade as the people lining up became hungry from what I later learned became a two-hour wait.

"That the line-up was for tickets to see *The Merry Widow* at the New Amsterdam I didn't realise until I turned the corner on 42nd Street. I learned later that the one ticket seller on duty when the box-office opened sent a runner to Mr. Savage urging that he find three more sellers to open every ticket window as quickly as possible."

The following Monday the company opened a week's tryout at the New Haven Theatre in Connecticut, a beautiful theatre ironically just about forty-five minutes from Broadway, that had then, and has many times since, seen the opening night of some of Broadway's biggest hits and most expensive bombs.

But there was no fear about *The Merry Widow* being a bomb! New Haven theatregoers, and many hundreds who travelled from New York to see this remarkable show that Alexander Woollcott had praised so colourfully, gave a standing ovation every night to the brilliant performances they saw.

The demand for tickets was so great that Henry Savage convinced Donald Brian and Ethel Jackson to add two matinee performances on Friday and Saturday.

"Even that first week people were selling tickets outside the theatre for five or ten times the original price," said Brian in 1943. "Reports reached us during the week that every seat at the New Amsterdam Theatre was sold out until well into 1908.

"It was an exhilarating time in my life. I was mobbed arriving and leaving the theatre. I signed thousands of autographs during the New Haven week. I tired my right arm so much that by Friday, in one scene where I was called on to raise my arm and point to a high window, I couldn't raise it above my shoulder the pain was so great. Ethel realised the problem and pointed her arm at the window. Next night we changed our positions onstage so that I could use my left arm onstage and thus continue signing autographs offstage with my right. I would have found it impossible to refuse the people who had given me such unexpected happiness."

10 The King of Broadway

The entire *Merry Widow* company arrived back in New York on Sunday, October 13, 1907, anticipating a peaceful week of final rehearsals at the New Amsterdam before the scheduled October 21 opening.

A brief story in the *New York World* said the show ran an hour over its expected time on the Monday opening in New Haven, but by Saturday it was running for two hours and thirty minutes, only ten minutes more than Herbert Savage, the producer had planned.

Although it was an unwritten rule that critics did not write about the out-of-town tryout weeks because many a bomb in New Haven was restaged to become a big hit in New York, no one told the company that on Saturday, October 12, the *New York Times* ran a story about the show's amazing reception in New Haven. The paper added that no seats were available at the New Amsterdam until February 1, 1908, and that seats would be available for shows after February 1, as soon as the tickets were printed.

The writer ended the story by telling his readers the time, 2:00 p.m., when the special train carrying the company would arrive at the New York Central and New Haven Railroad terminal the next day.

"We had not read the Saturday *New York Times* so we were not prepared for the thousands who met the train," said Donald Brian in 1943. "Nobody had thought to alert the police department and it was obvious there was no way we could get through the cheering crowds alive.

"Fortunately for us, the alert stationmaster led us through a baggage tunnel and out of the station through an emergency door. He had sent somebody ahead to alert the hansom cabs that were waiting to pick us up outside the front of the station that we would now be coming out of the back street entrance.

"When the crowd saw the cabs moving and sensed we were getting away, they followed them round the corner. But we jumped aboard in record time and the drivers tried to get the cabs moving faster and faster as we were followed by a mob of cheering fans, mostly women, who fortunately were unable to catch up with us.

"It was a wild ride, but the drivers were able to take the entire company and stage crews directly to their homes and apartments.

"Nobody ever did tell me who paid for the cabs, but I gave my driver the biggest tip I've ever given anyone."

Rehearsals continued all week.

"It took the stage crew, who had been with us all week in New Haven, two days to get all the scenery and lighting in place. It was an extravagant show and they worked miracles getting everything ready for our first complete run through at the New Amsterdam on Tuesday, October 15 at 8:00 p.m.

"It was heartbreaking to eliminate any of the brilliant dialogue or cut down on the time of musical numbers, but by 11:00 p.m. on Saturday, October 19, when we ended our final dress rehearsal we had reached the agreed running time of two hours and twenty minutes.

"Fifteen minutes before the final dress rehearsal was scheduled to start, every light in the theatre went out. A number of overloaded panel fuses had blown. But we had the best technicians in the city and in less than ten minutes the lights were back on again.

"There were many glitches during that final dress rehearsal on October 19, but nobody was worried. It has always been a tradition in the theatre that a good dress rehearsal is the foreteller of a bad opening night. We had so many stoppages during that rehearsal that we had no doubt our opening night would be perfect. And it was!

"But we had underestimated audience reaction and ran twenty-five minutes over our expected time. Time after time the audience came to its feet applauding. At the final curtain they applauded for more than fifteen minutes. I have since read other reports that said the final applause lasted twenty-five minutes or even half an hour, but our stage manager told me it was fifteen minutes and I have always accepted that as being accurate.

"A most wonderful thing happened as the entire company assembled onstage for the final curtain call. Everything possible you can imagine was thrown onstage. When the curtain finally went down, and stayed down, and we were able to relax onstage basking in the astonishing thing that had just happened to us, the stage crew picked up more than $200 in gold coins that we told them to share equally among all the non-performers.

"Next morning I was told the final tally of gifts was two dozen top hats, nine walking canes, some gold topped, more than twenty bonnets from the ladies, dozens of handkerchiefs, flowers and more than eighty bouquets – where did they hide them during the show – and right at my feet a pair of panties that so far as I could ascertain were the first ever thrown onstage at any performer.

"Someone picked the lacy garment up for me and I noticed a name and address embroidered on the panties. I can still remember every word clearly, but I have never told anyone from whom this very personal token arrived. Since I made no attempt to contact her, I have no real idea of her thoughts behind this astonishing gift.

"Suffice it to say that she was a beautiful young New York debutante who only a year later married into the famed Astor family and went on to fame as the mother of a very important person. I kept the panties in a locked silver box in my dressing room as a good luck charm until the day I was married, and when that happened I knew the good luck I had long awaited really had arrived. So I burned them in the theatre furnace and the young lady's secret and identity will die with me."

On October 22, a *New York Times* front-page story about the play's opening had this headline:

New King of Broadway Crowned
At the New Amsterdam Last Night

Donald Brian: The King of Broadway

The reviewer at the paper said the words that George M. Cohan echoed twenty years later in his autobiography. He said, "Never in the history of Broadway theatre has one man received the adulation that was poured on the star of *The Merry Widow*, Mr. Donald Brian, many times throughout the evening and in ever increasing intensity as the show neared its final curtain. New York was his for the taking last night. His character may have been a prince, but long before the final curtain it was almost possible to visualize the crown of a king on his head.

"The waltz will never be the same again and I doubt if any other performer will ever be able to copy or equal the footwork displayed by Mr. Brian and his leading lady, Miss Ethel Jackson, throughout the show. As they swept up and down a huge double staircase with four feet twinkling as one I held my breath, but not one foot was misplaced as they whirled around in a dance so intense and stimulating that I had never seen its like before.

"I anticipate everyone in the city will soon by whistling and singing what President Theodore Roosevelt last night christened as *The Merry Widow Waltz*.

"I knew little of composer Franz Lehar until tonight. He has made obsolete every other type of music and opened a new door through which I hope other composers will enter to try to emulate his brilliance. To achieve this they will have to be very, very good."

The review ran for thirty-eight inches of prime space in the *New York Times*. It ended with three paragraphs in a separate box beside the review. George M. Cohan, who never missed an opportunity to see his name in the news, was the author.

"I will send my personal landau and white horses to Mr. Brian's apartment on 51st Street to transport him to the theatre every night this week at seven o'clock. He will drive from his home to Broadway then down through Times Square before turning into 42nd Street and the entrance of the New Amsterdam Theatre.

"I hope New Yorkers will turn out in the hundreds to greet Mr. Donald Brian, the unquestioned King of Broadway."

They did not turn out in the hundreds! They turned out on October 22, 1907, in numbers the *New York Times* estimated as being "in excess of 20,000."

"They waved top hats and bonnets at me," Donald Brian recalled in 1943. "The landau was full of roses before I reached the theatre. I remember deciding during the ride that the roses would be sent to the city hospital to brighten the lives of the patients. Waiting police officers helped me through the crowd and into the theatre through the front doors.

"It was a day I shall never forget, and although I accepted George M.'s offer of his landau every night that week, I was unprepared for the huge crowds that did not diminish, but grew in number every evening.

"On the second and subsequent nights I invited some of the dancers from the show to join me for afternoon tea at my apartment and each night at 7:00, I took two of them with me in the landau.

"I have always been very sentimental and I was in tears as I listened to some of the generous comments shouted from the crowd. The girls dabbed handkerchiefs to my eyes to cheers from the huge crowd. On the second night, we actually stopped the traffic in Times Square as crowds rushed into the roadway from both sides of the square. Happily, no one was hurt and hundreds of New York's finest made sure that didn't happen again.

"What had I possibly done to deserve such a reward?"

The *New York Times*, still basking in the glory of Alexander Woollcott's scoop, was not finished. For an entire week it ran interviews with Franz Lehar, Herbert Savage, Ethel Jackson and many other members of the company, including the theatre stage doorkeeper who said he had been given four "burly security men" to restrain over-zealous ladies who nightly fought to get backstage before, during and after each performance.

But it was not only ladies who tried to crash the stage door. On the opening night, a well-dressed gentleman also tried in vain to gain admission backstage after the final curtain fell.

He reported the incident to the *New York Post* a few days later. "I realise I am not yet as important as the current President of the United States, Mr. Roosevelt, and was rebuffed by security men who obviously had no idea who I was. Thanks to my good friend, Mr. Herbert Savage, I was able, next morning, to get an appointment to meet with Mr. Brian for a private supper at my hotel after the final curtain of the Friday night's performance.

"I don't think Mr. Brian, who was obviously overwhelmed with the adulation poured on him, realized who I was, but had simply agreed to my request for a meeting because he was so grateful to Mr. Herbert Savage to whom he said he was deeply indebted.

"I asked Mr. Brian if he had seen President Theodore Roosevelt receive the $500 from Mr. Cohan.

"When he said he had witnessed the exchange of money and that President Roosevelt had given the money to one of the chorus ladies to be shared among them, I commented that I would at sometime try to equal or better that agreeable moment."

'In what way could you better that sir?' asked Mr. Brian.

"I told him he evidently was not a politically motivated young man and that was ideal for an entertainer, but that in just a few months I would be replacing Mr. Roosevelt as the United States' twenty-seventh President.

"Donald Brian looked stunned. 'What did you say your name was sir?' he asked.

'William Howard Taft,' I replied. 'Did President Roosevelt ever invite you to the White House?'

"'No sir,' he replied.

'Then consider this as my official invitation to attend my White House inauguration ceremonies and you will sit next to me and Mrs. Taft at the official inaugural banquet.'

"I arranged my contract with Herbert Savage to allow me a week out during the after-Broadway tour of *The Merry Widow* when we would be in Boston so that I could attend the inauguration," recalled Donald Brian in 1943. "It was an exciting event and President Taft kept his promise. Wherever he went, I went, and at the end of the ceremonies the president invited me to stay on at the White House for a week. I attended all the meetings usually restricted to top government officials and I remember the president asking me to swear on a Bible that I would never divulge any of the secrets I heard. I have kept that promise and will never tell anyone the many intriguing, sometimes startling, things I learned during that remarkable week."

President William Howard Taft was the second of eight United States presidents that Donald Brian was to meet during his illustrious career on Broadway that continued for more than thirty years after his triumph in *The Merry Widow*.

Other newspapers picked up the title, King of Broadway, and theatre management added a golden crown to the life-sized drawing of Donald Brian outside the New Amsterdam Theatre. Several weeks later, the theatre reported that it had to replace the portrait five times in less than ten weeks. "They just vanish during the night," said Herbert Savage.

It is interesting to note that one of the missing portraits turned up at an auction of theatre memorabilia in New York in 1973. There were only two bidders before an elderly lady got the rather dog-eared treasure for $700. She declined to give her name, saying only, "It brings back a memory of when I was very young."

At the same auction one of the specially produced elaborate first-night programs of *The Merry Widow*, bearing what purported to be the signatures of Donald Brian, Ethel Jackson and Franz Lehar, sold for $9,000.

Years later, Herbert Savage reported to the *New York Post* about the ingenuity of a group of women who stole one of the pictures from under the nose of the security guard posted at the front of the theatre after four pictures had already been stolen.

"One woman slipped on the sidewalk and fell to the ground crying. A lady with her called to the guard for help. Like a good man he dashed over to be of assistance. He was only away a few moments before he realised the fallen girl was uninjured, but he was too late to save the photograph, which two other ladies, hidden round the corner of the theatre, jumped out and stole. The guard rushed down to Broadway, but the ladies and the photograph had vanished into the dark night."

The theatre manager next tried nailing the picture to a billboard in front of the theatre and placed a guard there every night to stop it from being stolen. He was given instructions that he was not to move from his post for anything less than an earthquake.

"But they had to replace the picture several more times during the run of the show," said Herbert Savage. "The lipstick kisses all over Mr. Brian's face were making it difficult for him to be recognized. The guard stopped the picture from being stolen, but said it was impossible to control the women who constantly kissed the life-size picture."

In 1934, when Donald Brian was first in Hollywood, he was introduced to Canadian-born actress Mary Pickford.

"I have to confess to you, Donald," she said, "that I was one of the people who, with a little aid from my friends, stole one of your pictures from the front of the theatre and kept it for many years before it was lost during my move to Hollywood. I was the girl who pretended to slip on the sidewalk. I have always considered this to be one of my finest moments of acting, but couldn't help spoil it all by smiling when I saw the other girls running away with the picture.

"I must also tell you that I, and many other young actresses and the elite of New York's young debutantes of that era, were among those who kissed your portrait outside the theatre."

She added, "May I now kiss you in person, Mr. Brian?"

"Even though my wife was standing by my side I willingly accepted what was considerably more than just a gentle kiss from Miss Pickford," he said with a smile.

On July 4, 1908 Donald Brian led a parade of chorus girls and boys from 51st Street to Times Square where a watching crowd estimated to be in the thousands blocked all traffic in and out of the Square.

The parade was organized to support the New York dancers who were still receiving as little as eight dollars a week for their work. Other performers, like Marie Dressler, who had tried to support the dancers' cause were blacklisted. For several years, they were unable to get work with any of the New York managements who banded together to keep out the stars they felt were acting unfairly and not in the interests of the Broadway stage.

Marie Dressler, in her autobiography, praised Donald Brian for his courage that finally won better contracts for the dancers.

"Donny was such a big star. *The Merry Widow* was the most successful musical ever to reach Broadway, and when I suggested to him they would never dare to blacklist him, he and I organized the parade that finally broke the management cartel and helped create Actors Equity. The new union had the power to organize a strike that would close every show on Broadway, if managements didn't agree to give better pay to the dancers and other small role performers.

"It needed great courage for Donny to stand up as he did. But it was his stature on Broadway that finally created Actors Equity."

After only nine weeks in *The Merry Widow*, Ethel Jackson asked Herbert Savage to be freed from her contract. He told this story to an unidentified weekly magazine, after the final curtain fell on the show in 1908:

"I have never enjoyed working with a better management than yours, Mr. Savage," she said. "I have been in love with Donald Brian since the day I met him, but I am exhausted, utterly exhausted. Whirling around the stage, up and down the staircase, trying to keep up with Donny's split second moves, knowing that I would never be able to compete with him, has so exhausted me that I am not sleeping at night, but I find myself falling asleep in the oddest places like restaurants or while waiting for a fitting to try on a gown. I had to find a new church because I fell asleep one Sunday in the middle of one of the minister's rather boring sermons.

"I think it is time someone else tried to keep up with Donny who must be the fittest man on Broadway. He constantly adds new steps to his already bewildering array of footwork, and if I am not released soon I will undoubtedly collapse one night onstage to the detriment of the show."

Herbert Savage reluctantly agreed to release Ethel Jackson and two weeks later Lois Ewell became Sonia, the Merry Widow.

Lois Ewell had been in the chorus of *Forty-five-Minutes from Broadway* and Donald Brian had singled her out for special attention.

"I knew she was too good for the chorus, but at that time didn't know how I could enhance her career," he said. "When Mr. Lehar came along with his enchanting music I knew I had to get her into the company even in a small role.

"I must admit I knew Ethel was getting exhausted, often I had to help her offstage, and several weeks before she pleaded to be released I had elevated Lois Ewell to be her understudy, and she and I rehearsed the role of Sonia every morning. When Ethel left, Lois was ready to take over the role. She was a great success."

Only six weeks later, Donald Brian was once again rehearsing another replacement. Lina Abarbanell, a well-known dancer and singer in the New York theatre world was recruited to take over the role of Sonia when it became obvious that like Ethel, Lois was getting exhausted.

"Lina and I rehearsed every morning and she too was ready when Lois asked to retire."

Lina Abarbanell lasted ten weeks before being replaced by Rosemary Grosz.

"I had brought Rosemary into the show after we became friends on the road tour of *Forty-five Minutes*. She obviously was a step above the average dancer and I helped prepare her as understudy for Lina. I was able to convince Herbert Savage to give her the role of Sonia when Lina asked to be allowed to retire. I had noticed that night after night while Lina and I were dancing that Rosemary was duplicating her steps offstage.

"She had been one of the young dancers who had lived in my apartment several times when work was scarce, and I had always admired her willingness to learn from me.

"Looking back now on those incredible months, I believe Rosemary was the most successful of all the excellent ladies who played Sonia. She survived for an incredible eighteen weeks before slipping onstage and spraining an ankle. She finished the *Merry Widow Waltz* that night, a very vigorous and demanding number, before she even complained about the pain in her ankle.

"In anticipation of a later need for new Sonias, Georgia Caine and I had been rehearsing several hours each day, so Georgia was able to take over onstage the next night.

"It soon became obvious that Georgia couldn't keep up the spirited pace of the show very long and a few days later, I started working with Ruby Dale.

"After only three weeks, Georgia asked to be released and Ruby took over. Happily she continued for seven weeks right through to the final performance, but we did have another understudy waiting in the wings. Wendy Blackmore only had a chance to appear on Broadway once, in a totally unexpected way, but when the show was moved to Boston for four weeks she was our first Sonia."

Just before the final night of the Broadway production of *The Merry Widow* Donald Brian suggested to Herbert Savage that the *Merry Widow Waltz* be given very special treatment on that closing night.

"Herbert had told me he had blocked off more than 800 seats for people he knew, including all the elite of New York, many star performers, and personalities including President Roosevelt and President-elect William Howard Taft, who wanted to be in the audience for the last show. So I suggested that the *Merry Widow Waltz* be repeated six times with each of the show's Sonias doing the dance in turn. That meant that I would have to go through the routine six times."

'That will be impossible,' said Savage. 'I wince each night as I see you do just one *Merry Widow Waltz*, but to do it six times might kill you. I don't believe you could do it.'

Donald Brian laughed in 1943 when he told how he convinced the producer to agree to his final performance marathon.

"I got all six Sonias together and hired a piano player in a rehearsal room to play the accompaniment so we could try to see if the feat was possible. Around the fifth chorus I began to believe that I had taken on an impossible task, but Rosemary whispered words to me that I remember to this day, 'Dear Donny,' she said as we danced, 'I have always loved you and believe you have some supernatural powers that will let you achieve this finale the way you so richly deserve.'

"Those words gave me the spur to finish the sixth dance and when we presented it onstage at the theatre next morning for Herbert Savage, Rosemary whispered four more words, 'You can do it!' and it suddenly seemed as though I did have the supernatural strength she had suggested the day before.

"When Herbert, with considerable reluctance, unenthusiastically agreed that we could do the finale as I had requested I walked over to Rosemary and had I not spotted the diamond ring on her finger would have asked her then to marry me. She obviously read my mind and though I didn't say a word, she looked at me."

'I do love you, Donny,' she said, 'but I have given my heart to another man.'

"A few months later, since her father had died a year earlier, I walked her down the aisle when she married into a prominent banking family in the city. We kept in touch and only last week I heard from her. She was announcing the arrival of her third grandchild. Her marriage was very successful."

In a story printed in the *New York Post* the day after the show closed, Herbert Savage is reported as saying, "I watched the *Merry Widow Waltz* every night marvelling at the energy and power exhibited by Mr. Brian. Doing the routine as he did with more and more inventive steps as the show's run progressed, I prayed nightly that he would survive to the final curtain. But six choruses? I told him he was suggesting the impossible, but he finally persuaded me. The audience last night was thrilled to see the endurance displayed by this totally amazing man.

"He not only finished the planned six choruses of the *Merry Widow Waltz*, but he added one more, signalling to the musical director to start the music again, as he grabbed the startled Wendy Blackmore from the wings and whirled her around, up and down the staircase, as easily as if he was doing the dance for the first time. He then danced offstage as though he had done nothing unusual. All seven *Merry Widows* then came back onstage to take a bow with him. Although it was not the show's finale, the uproar from the audience stopped the show for at least ten minutes."

In the chronicles of Broadway *The Merry Widow Waltz*, that final night of October 17, 1908 is still considered, ninety-seven years later, to be the most memorable of all Broadway's greatest last nights.

The great dancer, Rudolf Nureyev,, said this to the *New York Post* in 1985, when he was interviewed while making a film, *That's Dancing*. "I have in my possession a six-minute portion of a reel of silent film that displays the incredible footwork of Donald Brian, a dancer largely forgotten today, but a big star in the early 1900s," he said. "It was filmed, I believe, at the New Amsterdam Theatre in 1908, but was never shown in public to anyone.

"I had hoped that the amazing footwork of this dancer could have been used in this film with me trying to equal his remarkable moves. But I am told the film is in such bad state of repair that it cannot be used. It is a pity because in my entire career I have never seen a dancer so skilled."

No other clippings in the extensive Nureyev file in the Performing Arts Library of the Lincoln Centre in New York suggest that he ever mentioned Donald Brian's artistry again. Today no one in the New York theatre archives knows what happened to the film he had discovered or where it was found.

At no time in his career did Donald Brian ever say the film had been made, but at that era the only connection he had in the film industry was Sidney Olcott at the Kalem Film Company studio in New York. It is reasonable to assume that Olcott made the film at Brian's request at the New Amsterdam Theatre during the run of *The Merry Widow*.

Nowhere in the extensive files of the Kalem Film Company is there any record of such a film being made, and in 1985, Sid Olcott, dead for more than twenty-five years, was not around to ask.

In January of 1908, the group of dancing school operators in New York City banded together to seek the services of Donald Brian as a guest choreographer at their annual meeting. The group's president convinced Brian to attend their Sunday banquet and teach some of his unique steps to the teachers.

President Maude Willmott later said this to the *New York World*: "We quickly realized that even the best of us were unable to capture the speed and intricacy of his movements. He received a standing ovation, but we all agreed we had learned nothing from this man with the twinkling feet and unique routines. He is a gracious man, but surely not of this world. His footwork is astonishing."

A request from the *New York Times* in April of 1908 that Donald Brian appear at an important Sunday charity concert brought Lillian Russell back into his life.

"It turned out to be one of most regrettable moments of my life," said Brian in 1943. "The story is still repeated in theatrical circles so it will do no harm if I tell you now what happened.

"She had relented and agreed to work with me in one number if I would promise not to try to outshine her. Of course I agreed, for many people revered Miss Russell and I felt it would be unwise to try to out perform her. I even decided to let her get the most applause for the number we were asked to do together.

"The number succeeded beyond my wildest dreams, we both did our part to make it memorable without outdoing the other. At that moment I held Miss Russell high in my esteem. But she was to shatter that good opinion as we took a final bow. She held up her hand to stop the audience applauding.

'I must tell you,' she said, 'that I consider Donald Brian to be the greatest performer ever to appear on the Broadway stage. But I must share a secret with you: two years ago I had the pleasure of seeing a part of him that few, if any, others have ever seen. I offered to share my bed with him that night to see which of us would be the better performer. Remembering my view of him on that special occasion, I think he would have come out on top then too.'

It was an era when such things were not spoken about in public, and the stunned audience didn't know whether to laugh or applaud, so they did nothing. Brian and Russell left the stage together to total silence.

"I walked slowly to my dressing room in total embarrassment," said Brian. "I never saw Miss Russell again after that night and on the Monday following the concert was almost afraid to make my entrance onstage at the New Amsterdam. Whether they had not yet heard the distressing story from the charity concert or just genuinely enjoyed my work I will never know, but the applause was as good as usual at the Monday show of *The Merry Widow*. But it was weeks before I had completely recovered from what I today still believe was the greatest *faux pas* ever made on the New York stage."

Lillian Russell's career started to decline from that moment, and only two years later she had returned almost exclusively to vaudeville, more often than not in theatres far away from New York. In 1912, at the age of fifty-one, she retired completely from the spotlight to a home she had built in Pittsburgh. She never again appeared on Broadway and died in Pittsburgh almost forgotten on June 6, 1922. Her solid silver casket still lies inside a marble tomb in the Allegheny Cemetery. She is said to have designed the silver casket and the marble tomb herself two years before her death. Her funeral was a quiet one with no Broadway personalities attending.

When the curtain fell for the final time on *The Merry Widow* in 1908 it had never had a single seat empty in the theatre during its entire run.

"I decided to limit the run to 406 performances, then a record on Broadway, because we had a commitment to take the show to Boston for four weeks and frankly, I feared for the health of Donald Brian and of company members who excelled and exhausted themselves nightly trying to keep up with the incredible pace he displayed," said Herbert Savage to the *Green Room* magazine some years later.

"We had a week out before the Boston opening and I urged Donny to put his feet up and rest, but a friend told me he saw Donny out every morning taking batting practise with the Brooklyn baseball team. The man had limitless energy."

In Boston, the four-week stay was extended to twenty-eight weeks, more than double the length of any other show, drama or musical, had ever lasted in a city theatre until that time. There was a week's break in the middle of the run so Donny could accept the invitation from President Taft to attend his inauguration ceremonies.

During the Boston run that played to capacity audiences, Wendy, Lois, Georgia, Ruby and Rosemary appeared at alternate shows.

"Ethel and Lina had moved on to other musicals in New York and although both wanted to be with us in Boston, they were unable to get any time away from their new shows," said Brian in 1943.

Wendy Blackmore told the *Boston Globe* that she and the other Sonias needed the three-day break between appearances and the week for President Taft's inauguration. "We all stand at the back of the theatre to watch Donny with whoever is onstage that night doing *The Merry Widow Waltz,*" she said. "We wonder how Donny can do the waltz every night, and we all realize that we are so good onstage because he leads us into every move and doesn't let us put a foot out of place. The man is tireless and surely the most wonderful dancer in the United States."

Over the next twenty years, Donald Brian played the role of Prince Danilo no less than six hundred times. In 1912 he took the musical on the road, playing for forty-eight weeks in theatres from coast-to-coast. He and Herbert Savage put equal amounts of money into the production and shared what Savage later said were "very substantial profits" when the show finally closed in Boston after another four-week run. In 1915 and 1916 they repeated that success with another forty-week tour of *The Merry Widow*. In 1923 he appeared in Chicago with the show for seven weeks.

"Whenever there was talk of a revival it was obvious that without Donald Brian, the show would fail," said Herbert Savage. "When he played Prince Danilo for the final time in 1931 he was fifty-six years old, but onstage he still looked the youthful and immaculate Prince Danilo he created when he was thirty-two. He hadn't gained a pound in weight and his face was totally unlined. His acting, dancing and singing talents never diminished in quality or energy."

"When we were on tour in Chicago with the 1931 production, I was greeted one night after the show at the stage door by a very familiar face," said Brian in 1943.

'You think you recognise me don't you Mr. Brian?' the visitor asked.

'You look amazingly like a young lady I knew twenty-four years ago in New York,' I said. 'She was beautiful and you too are beautiful.'

'My mother was Georgia Caine,' said the visitor. 'My name is Georgia Wallace. You were at my mother's wedding when she married Charles Wallace. He now heads a large insurance company here in Chicago. You are in the picture of the wedding that is on the piano in our home. Sadly I must tell you mother was killed in a car accident seven years ago, but as I was growing up she talked about you many times and I couldn't resist coming to see you tonight.'

"That night we sat and reminisced in my hotel suite for more than two hours," he said. "I asked if she had any stage ambitions and was saddened when she said no, but delighted to hear she was a successful writer on the staff of Chicago's biggest newspaper. We never met again, but I think of her even today."

Donald Brian was asked one final time in 1942 to revive *The Merry Widow*. "I looked at myself in the mirror," he said, "Although I still weighed the same as I did when I was thirty-two, I had to accept the fact that I was sixty-seven years old. I was flattered but reluctantly declined. "I couldn't imagine the audiences, even if they were composed entirely of elderly ladies in wheel chairs, visualizing me as a vivacious and exciting Prince Danilo.

"And, to be very truthful, I was not at all sure at that time if I could then have survived even one chorus of the vigorous and very sensuous *Merry Widow Waltz*."

Asked, in 1943, if the original six Merry Widows went on to greater fame on Broadway, Donald Brian smiled. "Only one! Lina Abarbanell played the lead at least a dozen times in many musicals and comedies on Broadway. I remember attending her final show when she was starring, in 1921, with Lionel Atwill in *The Grand Duke*. She had invited me because she had a special surprise for me. After the show, while we dined together, she showed me a huge diamond ring on her finger. Her husband-to-be was an important family member and director of the Ford Automobile Company.

'I am getting married next week and want you to walk me down the aisle,' she said. 'My father is too ill to travel from my parents home in Buffalo. Will you do it please, Donny?'

"I was delighted to agree since I had attended the weddings of all the other Sonias. All found husbands while they were playing Sonia and none ever missed the theatre, opting instead to raise large families. I never heard of any of their children going into the theatre."

Before the final show of *The Merry Widow*, Donald Brian had invited the president-

11 Dancing School

Donald Brian's popularity never seemed to wane. In 1911 he starred in *The Siren* as the Marquis de Ravaillac. His co-star was Julia Sanderson, one of Broadway's most sought-after leading ladies.

"I loved every performance with Julia," he said in 1943. "She was probably the most talented performer I have ever been fortunate enough to dance and sing with."

That same year Donald Brian made another attempt to repay the many good things that had happened to him since his arrival in New York.

On July 4, 1911 he opened the doors to one of the most successful dancing schools ever to exist in the city. In 1943 he recalled that day:

"My school was written about in the *New York Times* and *New York World* about a week before it opened. The stories gave the school address at 40 East 40th Street and said I would be there to register potential dancers aged from twelve to sixteen at 9:00 a.m.

"I had found a caretaker and a cleaner to make sure the large rehearsal room I had leased was spotless when the first students arrived. I expected perhaps twenty, maybe even thirty young dancers to join the classes I planned. But when I turned the corner on to 40th Street I was astonished to see the street almost blocked by a huge crowd.

"I may have been the most popular dancer in New York at the time, but such a crowd was totally unanticipated. By the time the receptionist I had hired had logged the final name into the books, we had totalled more than 400 hopeful dancers. Since most were with at least one parent this more than doubled the crowd."

It took until after 10:00 in the evening of the first day for Donald Brian to talk to every potential student and watch each one display very briefly his or her dancing skills. At lunch and supper times he arranged for food to be brought in from a nearby restaurant and everyone enjoyed a half-hour break to eat the meals.

"By the time I had checked off the most likely candidates, I was left with more than a hundred. I reluctantly told the other 300 that they couldn't at the time be enrolled in the school. About 200 of these were out of the age limit range I had agreed to accept. The oldest, if I recall correctly, was a man in his late sixties, the youngest only four.

"Not a word had been said in the stories about my fees and some of the young people arrived clutching envelopes holding more than $100.

"It was late in the evening before my receptionist was able to gather together the hundred candidates to whom we agreed to give a month's tryout.

"One mother asked about the fees. She was stunned when I told her the cost of a two-hour dancing lesson, including singing too for those who had the potential, would be only one dollar. And when I added that for those unable to pay the fee, the one dollar charge would be waived, one young mother rushed across the room and showered me with kisses.

"After a month, we had the hundred whittled down to thirty. The youngest was twelve, the oldest sixteen. Of those thirty, I agreed to provide additional voice training to five.

"We decided that the dancing classes would be held Monday through Friday at 9:00 a.m. for two hours, and the vocal classes the same days from 1:00 to 3:00 p.m.

"We ended up with six in each class, originally sorted by ages, with each class getting tuition for one day a week. As time went by we changed that policy a little, sorting the students more by ability than age.

"After six months we decided to drop all fees, it was more trouble than it was worth keeping track of those who had paid the dollar.

Dancing School

"The vocal classes were individual, each one of the five chosen was given two hours a week. I had hired a rehearsal pianist and when we were ready to start less than a week later, I had a staff of five on my payroll each week.

"The dollar fee didn't even pay the rent on the rehearsal room, but I was earning good money and was able to bear the cost without any difficulty.

"The most satisfying result from the school was the fact that in the first three years more than thirty of my students were already working in the professional theatre."

One fascinating story Donald Brian never told anyone about the school of dancing was revealed in a biography of the great comedy actor, W.C. Fields.

"In 1913 Florenz Ziegfeld had approached me about appearing in his annual *Ziegfeld Follies* show on Broadway," Fields wrote. "I was only a juggler at that time, but put a lot of comedy into my routines and Flo thought I had potential.

"But he told me I was clumsy and that every person in the *Ziegfeld Follies* had to be prepared to move with grace, and if necessary work with the dancers. He said he would want me to have enough control of my feet to walk up and down the staircase that was a feature of all his glamorous productions. 'Nobody as yet has ever fallen down,' he said. He told me to take dancing lessons and return to his office in three months.

"I was only thirty at the time and much slimmer than I am now in my Hollywood film days. A friend suggested I talk to Donald Brian who was then the biggest star on Broadway and considered by everyone to be the best dancer in New York City.

"I walked into Donny's 40th Street studio next morning and asked if he would consider me as a student. He had no idea who I was and I remember he laughed and said I was rather old to be taught to dance. However, when he heard my story he said if I would come to the studio every morning at 11:00 he would work with me for an hour.

"I wasn't very flush with money in those days and told Donny I couldn't pay more than ten dollars for each hour of training. He laughed and told me that money was not the most important thing in the world and that he admired my ambition to work in the *Follies*. 'The training will be free,' he said.

"I worked with Donny for three months before venturing back into Flo Ziegfeld's office on Broadway. I danced for half an hour onstage for Flo without any piano accompaniment and he hired me on the spot for his next *Follies*.

"Donny Brian's dancing lessons made my juggling act much better since I was able to tap while I juggled. The weird part of this story is that in the six years I worked with Flo Ziegfeld, and the two years with Earl Carroll's Vanities and George White's Scandals, none of those important people ever asked me to do a dance with the chorus line. But I did create a great act of my own with dancing and juggling everything from knives to flaming torches and, in 1929, Earl Carroll, who had moved to Hollywood to open a theatre there, asked me to join him as star of his nightly show.

"It was that move that gave me my first break in the movies, so it would be fair to say that Donny Brian is entirely responsible for all the money I have earned in Hollywood that has more than kept me in supplies of essential booze, and he never charged me a cent."

W.C. Fields, then a major name in Hollywood, was able to repay that generosity when Donald Brian first came to California in 1934. But that happy anecdote comes much later in Donald Brian's life story.

12 The Brooklyn Dodgers

Donald Brian continued his regular keep-fit batting practice with the Brooklyn Dodgers. By 1910 they had abandoned the name Brooklyn Superbas and a later title, the Brooklyn Robins, in favour of the Dodgers.

A new owner arrived on the scene in 1911. Charles Ebbets saw a future in baseball that few others did at that time. He announced that he had purchased land in Flatbush, a part of Brooklyn, and planned to build a 30,000-seat stadium there for the Dodgers in time for the start of the 1913 season.

Charles Ebbets, an avid theatregoer, soon became firm friends with Donald Brian. Ebbets notified everyone that Brian was, if he wished, to be permitted to take part in batting practice every morning when the team was in town.

In return Donald Brian persuaded friendly theatre managements to give Ebbets and his wife the two best seats in the house for the opening of every new show on Broadway.

The Dodgers had a young batter named Casey Stengel, and he and Donald Brian became lifelong friends. Donald Brian's obvious batting and fielding abilities intrigued Stengel.

In 1922 when he was with the New York Giants, Stengel gave an interview to the *New York Times* sports editor, in which he revealed for the first time why the Dodgers suddenly became better fielders and batters around 1912 or 1913.

"I asked Donny Brian if the entire team could come down to his dancing school to learn the reason why he was always able to turn on a dime and keep perfect balance when he was batting.

"Donny agreed and for the entire season of 1912 we attended dancing lessons at 11:00 in the morning three days each week. We didn't wear those skimpy outfits the regular dancers wore and we must have looked rather silly towering over the heads of the youngsters who often stayed on after their own lessons to see us making idiots of ourselves.

"I remember one of our pitchers, Cliff Curtis, who was several inches above six feet, getting so enthused that he was whirling the young students around over his head. Fortunately there were no accidents.

"Everybody had a great time and Charles Ebbets gave free tickets to the students so they and their parents could attend every Dodger game if they wished. One member of the team, an infielder, became so good after taking Donny's lessons that in 1913, he didn't make a single error all season.

"They didn't sing the *Star Spangled Banner* then as they do now before every game, and then Charles Ebbets invited Donny to sing it at the opening game in 1913, when we had moved into the new Ebbets Field, I believe it was for the first time.

"Donny not only taught his regular students how to dance, he gave them vocal lessons too, and everyone applauded loudly as they all walked on the field with Donny who used some kind of a megaphone to sing our national anthem.

"Soon every baseball club had a singer or band before each game and though the Yankees and Giants tried to lure Donny away, he would not sing for anyone other than the Dodgers.

"Donny threw out the first ceremonial ball on that special occasion when Ebbets Field was opened. It whistled right across the plate. If I'd been at the plate, I could have hit that one for a homer.

"When Ebbets Field was first opened, the left field boundary was 419 feet from home plate and centre was 477 feet. I can't remember the right field distance, but it was much more than 400 feet and ended at a huge scoreboard. If you could hit the scoreboard, you got a home run. Before the first game Donny was taking batting practice and he had a huge hit that not only reached the scoreboard, but also struck an advertising sign on the scoreboard that offered a free suit to anyone who hit that particular spot. I remember Abe Stark, the tailor who owned the space, refused to give Donny a suit because he said it only applied to hits during an actual game. I don't believe anyone other than Donny ever hit that sign, so Abe didn't have to give away a single suit.

"I did get a home run in that first game on April 5, 1913, when we beat the newly christened New York Yankees 3-2. But my home run was an inside the park homer as I ran around the bases when the Yankees outfielder, who I won't shame now by naming, let the ball go over his head and it rolled to the wall at the 477 foot mark. I had all the time in the world to trot around the bases, even doing a few of the steps I learned from Donny on each base pad."

Donald Brian added something extra to Stengel's story. "George M. Cohan used to go with me to some of the games and when he heard Charles Ebbets asking me how we could help create more interest in the team, he suggested that one of the team be made into an odd character who would attract newspaper and hopefully the public's attention.

"George M. suggested Casey Stengel. He said his gruff voice and rather sly but likeable smile would make him the perfect candidate. He volunteered to write some rather unusual statements for Casey to repeat as often as possible in public. 'And make sure members of the press hear them,' he added.

"Casey Stengel loved the idea. And over the years that followed he came out with some amazing humorous comments, which the newspapermen and readers all thought came from his fertile mind. In reality, every one was written for him by George M.

"I remember one of these remarks to this day. It was Cohan's wit delivered by Stengel. This is what Casey came out with at a special banquet at which he was asked to speak. 'There comes a time in every man's life, and I have had plenty of them,' said Stengel. The audience roared and Casey became very adept at looking embarrassed at his blunders. He was a very sharp person and far from being the tongue-tied man that George M. made him out to be with his one-liners.

"After George M. died last year (1942), Casey has never come out with another good line."

Stengel died at the age of eighty-five in 1975 in Glendale, California. Several books were written about him and his witticisms, but not one writer ever knew about or thought to mention George M. Cohan's part in his success.

In 1913 Donald Brian opened as star of *The Marriage Market*. Again his show was the hit of the Broadway season. It seemed nothing Donald Brian could do would lessen his popularity.

The baseball season was over and Charles Ebbets and every one of the Dodger players were seated in the theatre when the curtain went up on opening night.

"Mr. Ebbets thought it would be effective if we all went in our baseball uniforms," said Stengel. "It was written about next day and talked about for months and we signed hundreds of autographs for members of the audience. Donny didn't know we were to attend, but at the end of the show when he took his applause he held up his hand and told the audience that if they requested it, by applauding, the greatest baseball team in the world would join him onstage. Everyone in the theatre stood up and cheered, including me. That was perhaps the funniest and most embarrassing spontaneous moment of my life.

"Donny actually taught us all two or three dance steps in the few minutes we were onstage, but I'm not sure to this day if we were a success or the laughing stock of the city. But it was a lot of fun."

13 Harry Houdini

During the run of *The Marriage Market*, Harry Houdini, the master illusionist, then drawing huge crowds to vaudeville theatres around North America visited Donald Brian. This is how Donald Brian recalled, in 1943, that 1913 visit:

'Mr. Brian,' said Houdini, 'I have a suggestion for you that I think may prove to be challenging. I would like you to appear with me at the Palace Theatre on Broadway in a vaudeville show. Does that intrigue you, Mr. Brian?'

"I remember asking Harry Houdini who would get top billing he or I," said Brian. "He had an answer that was definitely intriguing.

'On the marquee outside the theatre I have devised a method of electric lighting that will show my name, then fade and your name will replace it. On all the posters and advertising material we will split fifty-fifty. Your name will be top on half the posters, mine will be top on the other half.

'I will pay you $2,000 each week of the four-week run. You will hire at my expense twelve dancers: six male, six female, and will do a thirty minute spot with them to close the first half of the show. You may sing, dance and do anything else you wish.

'I will take over the entire second half of the show until the finale when I shall call on you to take another bow onstage. I will then tell the audience that you have consented to take part in one of my illusions. I will say I plan to put you in the wooden packing case, which my assistants will, at that moment, be carrying onstage. You will step inside the trunk, which will be nailed shut, and then be raised to ten feet above the stage. When the packing case falls apart high in the air, you will have vanished.

'Then I will say that no theatre magic is greater than yours, Mr. Brian, and that I will call on you to reappear. A spotlight will be put on a seat in the third row of the orchestra stalls. I have chosen that because the third row seats are viewable from every other seat in the Palace including the top balcony. You will rise from that seat and join me onstage to what I anticipate will be thunderous applause. We will bow together and walk off together sharing what I predict will be a standing ovation.

'You have been a Broadway star now for almost a decade, but I venture to suggest that my idea will even surpass any success stories you have accomplished to date. You will be the most talked about person in New York. How does that intrigue you, Mr. Brian?'

"I was completely and instantly sold on the idea," said Brian. "Did he hypnotize me into agreeing? Some papers suggested he did, but that is not true. I loved the idea and couldn't wait to begin rehearsals."

Opening night at the Palace Theatre brought standing ovations to Donald Brian for his superbly created dancing and singing act, and to Houdini for his many remarkable illusions that stopped the show with their originality.

As Harry Houdini predicted, the final illusion worked every night. The reappearance of Donald Brian in the third row of the orchestra seats brought gasps from the crowds. Ovations followed this finale as Houdini and Brian shook hands and walked off to opposite sides of the stage.

But Donald Brian was never one to miss the opportunity to be in the biggest spotlight.

"I contacted a magic store in New York run by another illusionist and had a special suit made for the final trick. When Harry shook hands with me onstage, in the finale of the show, my entire hand came away in his. Even Harry said it was a clever trick. As he stood there holding what appeared to be my hand, he agreed it was a great finale. He looked at the apparently empty sleeve and made a remark I will never forget.

'Brilliant Donald,' he said. 'Now I shall have to learn how to sing and dance like you.'

Harry Houdini

"He held out his left hand to shake my left hand and as we shook hands, I realised Harry had improved on my trick. I was left holding a realistic spongy hand and some liquid like blood was coming out of the hand and his empty sleeve. For a moment, the audience gasped then roared with laughter and applause.

"Obviously the illusionist I had worked with had tipped Harry off to my plan and he proved that he was indeed the greatest illusionist in the world.

"At that moment, Harry pointed to the stage box on his left. As the house lights went up I saw that President Woodrow Wilson was sitting in the box. I would never have dared risk using the empty sleeve trick if I had known he was to be there.

"After the show, the president came backstage and I was introduced to my third United States president. I still recall his greeting as he put his hand out. 'I am not sure what I have left to shake,' he said, 'but I would like to say thank you for a superb evening of entertainment.'

"Our teaming together brought many theatregoers who had previously shunned vaudeville to the Palace Theatre. There were as many top hats, dinner jackets and fancy dresses there as I had ever seen in the legitimate theatre."

Asked many times how Houdini accomplished the trick that made him vanish, he always professed not to know. All he would ever say was that a member of Houdini's stage crew sat in the third row seat until "Harry Houdini distracted the audience, a feat at which he was brilliant, and I was able to change places with the assistant in seconds without anyone noticing what was happening."

How he got out of the packing case, or where he went when he did get out, he never revealed to anyone.

Donald Brian many years later told his wife how Houdini made him vanish and reappear in the audience, but she never mentioned it to anyone. In 1943 they both said in unison, "Houdini's secret is safe with me."

The Society of American Magicians honoured Donald Brian on Tuesday, November 30,

1926. Harry Houdini had collapsed and died on October 31 in Detroit while he was appearing in the city's largest theatre. His death followed an unfortunate accident in a Montreal theatre a week earlier in which he was injured during one of his illusions.

"I was invited to the Houdini Memorial Night in the East Room of the Hotel McAlpin, on Broadway at 34th Street, to talk about my friendship with Harry.

"The Society had a strict rule that would not allow any person to become a member who was not a practising magician, and when Harry put forward my name for membership in 1915, he taught me a trick that I could do at my acceptance meeting.

"I broke open a new pack of cards and asked the society's president, Bernard Ernst, to take any card and I would identify it immediately. He selected a card and before he had even looked at it I said it was the ace of hearts. He showed the card to the members and it was indeed the ace of hearts. From the generous applause I knew that I was to be accepted as a member.

"I am sure every magician in that room knew how to do the simple trick I had just performed, for they were kind enough not to ask me to do the trick twice. The second time would have given away the secret. Every card in the pack was the ace of hearts."

14 U.S. Army Said "No"

When World War I began in 1914, Donald Brian, who many people considered to be the fittest man in the United States, tried to enlist in the United States Army, but was turned down. Almost unbelievably the medical board report that rejected the thirty-nine year old dancer said he had "flat feet" which might prove to be a liability to the army, if he was called on to do long marches or be on his feet standing in the trenches for long periods of time!

Obviously none of the doctors who examined him had been in the audience at the New Amsterdam Theatre to see his spectacular dancing on the last night of *The Merry Widow.*

Donald Brian decided to serve the United States in a different way. "I got together a small company of singers, dancers and comedians and we toured more than one hundred of the recruiting camps playing in tents, mess halls, and often the open air," he said in 1943.

"It was a special thrill for me because I found that more than the wealthy New Yorkers liked my performances."

What he didn't say was that he personally paid the salaries, meals and all other expenses of the entire company for almost three months.

It was revealed in George M. Cohan's autobiography that Donald Brian had insisted in each contract he signed during the war that every night twenty of the best seats in the theatre must be reserved for United States military personnel, and that no charge was ever to be made for the seats. The tickets were distributed by service organizations in the city.

On August 24, 1914 Donald Brian opened in a new musical, *The Girl from Utah* at the Knickerbocker Theatre. Donald Brian bought ten seats in the front row of the dress circle for each of the first six nights "because from there, the audience can see our dancing most clearly." He gave these away free to the students of his dancing school and their parents.

George M. Cohan recalled in his autobiography: "Since many of the students and their parents had little money, he arranged for them all to go to an upscale clothing store in the city to be outfitted in clothing that would not let them look or feel out of place among the elite of New York sitting in the seats next to them. Donny, of course, paid the bill."

In 1915 he was playing the Grand Duke in *Sybil*, once again with Julia Sanderson and the great stage character actor, Joseph Cawthorne. Again, the musical was a big hit, and the *New York Post* told its readers that since Donald Brian's 1907's *Merry Widow* triumph, not one seat had ever been vacant at any of his later productions including the current hit, *Sybil*.

"I was very impressed by one young lady who came to my school for singing and dancing lessons in 1915," he said in 1943. "She was about thirteen at that time and I gave her extra hours of training because I was impressed by her grace, even at that age, and her dedication to the new art she was learning. I saw a great future for her in the professional musical theatre, but never dreamed at that time that I would later be the one to put an end to that career."

When she was only fifteen in 1917, he got Virginia O'Brien a small role in the Knickerbocker Theatre production of *Her Regiment*, a musical in which he was starring. She danced in one number alone with Donald Brian, a number that stopped the show every night.

In 1918 when Brian was appearing in *The Girl Behind the Gun* at the New Amsterdam Theatre he requested she be given the small supporting role of Zellie. But when the leading lady, Wilda Bennett, was taken ill one evening just before curtain time, and the show was about to be cancelled, Virginia O'Brien volunteered to take over the role.

U.S. Army Said "No"

The next day the *New York Post* said, "Miss O'Brien, only sixteen years old, stepped out from her small role in the production to take over the leading lady role vacated through the illness of Miss Wilda Bennett.

"Her youth, vitality and charm almost stole the show from the veteran star, Donald Brian, a feat not easily accomplished. At the final curtain, Mr. Brian led her down to the front of the stage, bowed to her and backed up stage so she alone could take the applause she so rightly deserved."

Three days later Wilda Bennett returned to the company. On the night of her return, she brought Virginia O'Brien to the front of the stage at the final curtain and presented her with a huge bouquet of roses handed up from the audience by one of the theatre ushers.

Virginia O'Brien returned, without complaining, to her small role in the show. *The Girl Behind the Gun* had taken Donald Brian back to the New Amsterdam Theatre, the scene of his first triumph. It was a major success, running 160 performances.

Later in the run, Virginia O'Brien twice more took over the role played by Wilda Bennett when she was indisposed. On one of these occasions, George V. Hobart, writer of several successful shows on Broadway, spotted her.

After the show ended that night he came backstage to see Donald Brian. "Donny," he said, "I would like you to read the script of my new musical, *Buddies*. The Selwyn brothers have agreed to finance the production and it will be staged at their new Selwyn Theatre. I think this musical is perfect for you, and with your permission I would like to suggest to the Selwyns that Miss O'Brien be your leading lady."

"It was mention of Virginia that created my enthusiasm at first; I had slowly realised that I was falling in love with this talented and beautiful singer and dancer. The two of us working together might help satisfy both of us that perhaps we were meant for each other."

Donald Brian read the script of *Buddies* and fell in love with that too.

"The Selwyns asked if I knew an actor named Ralph Morgan," he said in 1943. "I had indeed seen him in a play called *Under Cover* in 1915 with Lucile Watson. I had also met him much earlier when I negotiated my first contract with Herbert Savage for *The Merry Widow*. He had been a lawyer at that time, but shortly afterwards followed his illustrious brother Frank into the acting profession. Frank Morgan will always be remembered for his many film appearances, particularly the character of the Wizard in the *Wizard of Oz* in 1939. I thought Ralph would be perfect for the role of Babe in *Buddies*.

"Very quickly it was agreed that I, Virginia and Ralph would star in the show. The contract was very lucrative and I made sure Virginia got excellent money for her first big contract.

"But *The Girl Behind the Gun* was playing to capacity audiences and didn't seem to be slowing down at all. I wasn't sure how long Archie Selwyn would wait for us, but luck was once more on my side. The New Amsterdam owners, never dreaming our show would still be going strong and nearing 150 performances, told us we had to be out of the theatre by October 5, 1919, as they had a commitment for a new show there to open on October 27.

"I was sorry to see the end of *The Girl Behind the Gun*, but found myself getting more and more enthused about working with Virginia. I knew I was in love with her, but even after *Buddies* opened on October 27 at the Selwyn Theatre, and she became a star in her own right, I wondered how I, then forty-four years old, could possibly propose to a very youthful seventeen year old."

But *Buddies* had almost failed to open. Just before the first night at the Selwyn Theatre, Donald Brian was notified by Actors Equity, of which he was a founding member, that the union was preparing to strike all shows staged by managements who had refused to accept the new increased wage scale that they had presented. The Selwyn brothers were among the managements who had refused to agree to the new contract.

U.S. Army Said "No"

"I was horrified," said Brian. "Here was the union I had so gladly helped create now threatening to close down every show on Broadway.

"The New York theatre owners and producers and management companies got together and decided to defy the union. They claimed the new wage scale would force them to raise ticket prices and in that event it was likely some of the New York theatres and producers would go bankrupt.

"The new wage increase didn't affect the theatre's well paid star performers like me, Virginia and Ralph, but Archie Selwyn advised us that he could not possibly agree to raise the wages of the other thirteen members of the cast to the proposed new scale.

"When he advised Equity of this, they told us we would officially be on strike from the following Monday, which was our opening night.

"We knew we had a wonderful show and worked out what the increase in salaries would do to the bottom line every week. We told Selwyn that we would take the extra money for the thirteen lesser paid members of the cast out of our own pockets, if he would agree to meet the union demands.

"Selwyn pointed out that by agreeing he would also have to raise salaries of all the cast members in his two other shows running at that time. He said the stars of the other shows were not as willing as us to reduce our salaries to help those underpaid.

"We were facing a strike I believed was for good reasons, but didn't want to lose *Buddies*. Ralph Morgan, who had been a lawyer before becoming an actor, suggested a way out. 'Buy the show,' he said.

"We told Archie Selwyn that we were prepared to purchase all rights to *Buddies* from him for $150,000 dollars. In addition we would give him, as the theatre owner, 20 percent of the box-office receipts every week as rent so he could pay the front-of-house staff not affected by Equity. I put up $100,000, Virginia and Ralph each invested $25,000."

Virginia O'Brien laughed in 1943 at that statement. "Donny," she said, "aren't you forgetting to say that you gave me the $25,000 so I could buy my share?"

"That was probably the best investment I ever made," he said. "If *Buddies* had been cancelled, our lives might have been very different.

"As the owners of the actual show," Brian continued, "we were then a management company. If we chose to increase the salaries of the thirteen underpaid performers to the new Equity rates the union could not force us to go on strike.

"We notified Equity of our decision and since we complied with their new deal we were allowed to open on October 27, 1919. A lot of other theatres were closed and the Selwyn Theatre turned away hundreds at the box-office every night. Even when we added an extra matinee each week, and became the first Broadway musical ever to play six nights and three matinees, we played to capacity audiences. It was a very successful show.

"By agreeing to their new contract we had not defied the union and it wasn't long before other managements also agreed to the Equity salaries. And within six months, the new agreement was ratified by every production company in the city.

"But we were the first management group to accept the new salary scale, something I have been proud of all my life.

"Our $150,000 investment made myself, Virginia and Ralph wealthy. It added a great deal to Selwyn's existing riches and everyone was happy. In a unique way, we had forced other managements to give a break to the underpaid performers."

Buddies ran for an astounding 259 performances, almost two thirds of the record run of *The Merry Widow*. At that time on Broadway, with few members of the city's theatre audiences coming from communities more than fifty miles from New York, it was considered a resounding success. In those days, there were few tourists in the city to keep shows running indefinitely, as they do today.

Once again the *New York Times* said, "The King of Broadway is holding tight on to his crown. With a cast of only sixteen, this fascinating musical comedy has none of the glamour of his earlier successes, but as an audience pleaser it will be hard to equal by any other drama, comedy or musical in the 1919 season.

"Donald Brian seems unable to put a foot wrong in his choice of shows in which to star."

The review went on to praise the talented Ralph Morgan and delighted Donald Brian with its closing paragraphs.

"But it was a relative newcomer to the Broadway stage who really challenged Donald Brian for audience appreciation. I have never seen Virginia O'Brien before, but hope to see a great deal of her in the future.

"Her total enthusiasm for every line, every song, every dance step was infectious. I saw a look in her eyes that seemed to be saying to Mr. Brian, 'Can you do any better?'

"When the final curtain fell and we had to reluctantly accept the fact that this wonderful evening was over, Mr. Brian did what many a lesser performer might have hesitated to do, he called Miss O'Brien down to the footlights when he was taking his final bow as star of the show.

"As a child, I was threatened with deafness and had learned to lip read so was able to understand what Mr. Brian and Miss O'Brien whispered to each other when he put out his hand to greet her. This was their brief conversation:

> Miss O'Brien: 'Donny, this is your show, I really shouldn't be down here with you.'
>
> Mr Brian: 'Indeed you should, this was your night as much as mine. I hope we will have more nights like this in future.'
>
> Miss O'Brien: 'Yes, please, Donny.'

"This show will run for a long time. Better book your seats now."

In 1943, Virginia O'Brien in Hollywood with her husband, but retired as an actress, recalled the review.

"Every word is engraved in my head," she said. "The reviewer was wrong about one thing. The look in my eyes was trying to tell Donny that I was waiting for him to propose marriage to me.

"The show closed on June 12, 1920, my eighteenth birthday. Of course there were the usual gifts handed up over the footlights, but not the one I really wanted. I hoped Donny would slip an engagement ring on my finger and tell me we were to be married."

"But I couldn't," said Donald Brian. "I just looked at this beautiful young eighteen year old and couldn't imagine why she would possibly want to marry a forty-five year old.

"But I did want to marry you," she said. "I wanted it more than anything else in the world. If I had walked out of the theatre knowing I would never appear anywhere again, I would have been happy if marrying you would have been the end of my acting career. Forty-five? You looked and acted like a very youthful twenty-five year old."

"Look at me now," said Donald. "You are still beautiful at forty-one, but here I am, a character actor, sixty-eight years old."

"Not to me," said Virginia. "I was only thirteen when I asked to join your dancing school. I thought you were wonderful then, and I still do today."

But, in 1920, it was almost six more years before Virginia O'Brien finally heard the words she had waited to hear.

The next season both Donald Brian and Virginia O'Brien were asked to appear in a revival of the very popular musical, *The Chocolate Soldier*.

It had originally opened in September 1909, to considerable acclaim, but lost out at the box-office to Donald Brian's success in *The Dollar Princess*.

U.S. Army Said "No"

"We never saw the show in 1909," said Donald. "I don't think Virginia had seen any show at that time, she was only seven, and the matinees for *The Chocolate Soldier* were always scheduled for the same days, Wednesday and Saturday, as *The Dollar Princess* and we were still running when it closed."

In a history of Broadway, written by Alexander Woollcott, he tells the story of Donald Brian and Virginia O'Brien's first contact with Lee Shubert, one of the most respected impresarios in New York.

"The two performers walked unannounced into Lee Shubert's office at the Century Theatre and asked for the roles of Lieutenant Bumerli and Nadia Popoff in *The Chocolate Soldier*.

"Lee Shubert told me his jaw dropped open," wrote Woollcott.

'This is a revival, Mr. Brian,' said Shubert. 'You are the biggest star on Broadway. We can't hope to pay the sort of money you would expect. We only plan to run for twelve weeks. What sort of money would you consider working for?'

'It was Virginia O'Brien who answered,' said Shubert.

'We would work for a percentage of the gross box-office receipts,' she said.

'Donald Brian looked at her rather slyly, but said not a word,' said Shubert. 'Then I believe we can come to an agreement. Do you have an agent to whom we must talk?'

'I think we can settle things right now,'" said Donald. 'Give us 20 percent of the box-office between us and you can draw up the contracts.'

'I rose to my feet,' said Shubert, 'I put out my hand somewhere between the two of them not knowing whose hand to shake. They both clasped it together.'

'I have long been aware that you are the greatest performer on the Broadway stage,' Shubert said to Donald Brian, 'and I have been told that at no time in the history of all your musical successes has there been a bad word between you and the managements for whom you have worked. Now I know those words to be true. I am certain we will all have a good relationship.'

Donald and Virginia left the office, planning to meet the next day to sign the contracts. Lee Shubert, in his memoirs, remembers saying to his secretary, "Julie, I believe those two are secretly married. What a team."

The Chocolate Soldier was another Broadway success for both Donald Brian and Virginia O'Brien. Both received wonderful reviews and once again, the Century Theatre was packed from opening to closing night on February 18, 1922.

Warren G. Harding had been inaugurated as President of the United States in 1921, and later that year he sat in the president's box at the Century Theatre to see *The Chocolate Soldier*. After the performance, he came backstage.

"Mr. Brian," said President Harding, "I normally eat before visiting any theatre, but tonight decided to risk being very hungry until after show because I understand professional entertainers do not eat before a performance. So before I collapse from hunger, I would like to invite you Mr. Brian, and your wife (he nodded to Virginia) to join me in my New York hotel suite for a supper I think you will find particularly interesting, perhaps even stimulating."

"It would be an honour, sir," said Donald. "My wife and I will be delighted to join you."

"I remember smiling like the Cheshire cat that had found a bowl of cream," Virginia said in 1943. "I looked at Donny with a great big smile that I thought might bring a response, but it didn't. That night I found being addressed as Mrs. Brian was highly satisfying, but Donny rather shyly ignored the situation. I wondered what on earth I could do to let him know being Mrs. Brian was exactly what I wanted."

The president's special treat for Donald Brian was a dinner of fresh salmon that he said his staff had obtained from a vessel that brought fresh fish from Newfoundland to New York. "It was one of only two they had caught in the waters off your home country," said the president. "I sent the other direct to the White House and when I eat it I shall think of the pleasure I had dining with you and your beautiful wife this evening."

"The president had a luxurious car and driver waiting outside the hotel to take us, after the supper, to what he presumed was our apartment," said Virginia. "Actually it was Donny's on 51st Street and when the car left, Donny walked me over to my apartment on 49th Street.

'Goodnight, Mrs. Brian,' he said, bowing charmingly before walking back to 51st Street.

"I got a little hope that night. I watched 'til he disappeared and noticed he did quite a few intricate dance steps on his way home. I sensed that perhaps he too was happy about our deception.

"*The Chocolate Soldier* was so successful that the Shuberts asked if we would be willing to go on a twenty-week tour of major theatres from Washington to Los Angeles.

"While we were in *The Chocolate Soldier* in New York, Donny received a wonderful offer from producer William Brady to star in a new musical, *Up She Goes*," said Virginia.

"But it was not scheduled to open until November so we accepted when Mr. Shubert offered us 30 percent of the box-office and a private first class rail coach to take us and the other members of the company from city to city. It was a wonderful tour, and when we reached Washington, President Harding sent an invitation to the theatre inviting Mr. and Mrs. Donald Brian and the entire cast to dine with him and Mrs. Harding at lunchtime on the Thursday.

"Donny never objected to the Mr. and Mrs. tag on the invitation, so I said nothing. But he felt our musical director and the five-man stage crew, who travelled with us, should also be included in the invitation.

"Would you believe he called the White House and got right through to the president? He suggested to President Harding that these important members of our touring group should not be forgotten, and the president said that would be completely acceptable.

'The table will be set for these additional six important people,' he said.

"Donny and I talked about those days recently and agreed that today if such an invitation was offered, the actors would probably be living together on the tour, married or not, but in 1922 that didn't happen, at least not to Donny and I."

Up She Goes opened on November 6, 1922, and Virginia recalled how delighted she was to see a paragraph in one of the many excellent reviews that read like this: "Mr. Brian will undoubtedly be very busy in this new show for the foreseeable future, and it is a pity there was no role written for his wife, Virginia O'Brien. They made such a perfect team in *The Chocolate Soldier*. Hopefully Mrs. Brian has not retired at so youthful an age and that soon we will see her on Broadway again."

Because there was no part in *Up She Goes* suitable for Virginia O'Brien, she accepted, with the blessing of Donald Brian, a role in *The Rise of Rosie O'Reilly*, a new musical written by George M. Cohan, scheduled to open at the Liberty Theatre on December 23, 1922.

In his autobiography George M. Cohan said, "Of course I knew that Donny and Virginia were not married, but never disillusioned the writers who were convinced this was the case. I was sure then that the wedding would happen sooner or later. To ensure Virginia came to no harm in my show, I hired Colleen Ross as her dresser because Colleen had at one time been a member of the New York Police Department. She had instructions from me to see Virginia home safely each night to her apartment and she did the job very effectively.

"It was only years later that I was told by Virginia that she knew exactly what I was doing and was grateful for the extra security. At that time in the New York theatre 'mashers' as they were called waited around the stage doors trying to pickup the good looking girls in the show.

"Many of these mashers were genuinely looking for wives and many were from good families, but many were not and very nasty stories about the behaviour of some of these mashers were widespread in the business."

The newspaper reviews for *The Rise of Rosie O'Reilly* were all good with Virginia O'Brien earning excellent comments from every paper.

When, in January of 1924, *Rosie O'Reilly* had a Friday matinee, an afternoon when *Up She Goes* was dark, Donald Brian was in the audience. At the final curtain she blew him a kiss from the stage. Donald Brian stood up and bowed.

The next day in one of the gossip columns that were springing up in every major New York daily newspaper, Walter Winchell had this to say:

> "Two lovebirds were reunited yesterday at the Liberty Theatre when Donald Brian attended the matinee to see his wife in *The Rise of Rosie O'Reilly*."

In 1943 Virginia O'Brien smiled at Donald Brian as she produced the clipping from a scrapbook. "Even then Donny didn't take the hint," she said. "We were man and wife in the eyes of presidents, writers and the general public, but he didn't suggest we might make it a reality. I couldn't believe that he was so oblivious of my love for him."

Donald Brian broke into the conversation. "That's a long time ago, my dear," he said. "You may as well know now that I was afraid to ask, in case you turned me down. You were twenty-one and I was forty-eight. I was a middle-aged man, you were starting what looked like being a very successful career."

"I would have married you if you had been seventy-eight," said Virginia. "I had not then, or have since, met a man so honest, kind and so totally loveable."

"Maybe you should have told me that twenty years ago," said Brian with a smile.

The Rise of Rosie O'Reilly lasted a very successful eighty-seven performances, and introduced Virginia O'Brien to a young chorus girl in the show who impressed her with the fastest tap dancing she had ever seen from a woman.

"The show marked the Broadway debut of Ruby Keeler who went on to great success on Broadway and later in Hollywood. We vowed to remain friends all our lives and I still talk to her on the phone for quarter of an hour each day," she said in 1943.

"I tried hard to convince her to refuse Al Jolson's proposal of marriage. I had seen the way Jolson carried on with the young girls in all his shows, but Ruby was so smitten by his insistence in courting her that she made the biggest mistake of her life and married him."

In a 1975 interview, a year after Virginia O'Brien had died in New York City, Ruby Keeler said, "She and Donny were the two most honest people in the world. They never had a cross word between them. They never shouted or argued other than in a civilized manner if they disagreed with someone's point of view.

"Donny would never allow me to publicize the tap lessons he gave me, and never charged a cent for his work. I only wish he could have still been alive to see me use some of his brilliant footwork when I returned to Broadway in 1972 to appear in *No, No, Nanette*.

"But Virginia, who had appeared with Donny in *No, No, Nanette* in 1923, was there and she shed a few tears in my dressing room after the first night show. I wanted to tell the newsmen who invaded backstage with cameras and notebooks who she was, but she said, 'No, my day is long past. This night is yours, Ruby. No other version of *No, No, Nanette* will ever be remembered after your triumph tonight. Tell them I am just an old friend.'

"When Donny died at their home in Great Neck, New York, in 1948, it was fortunate that she had her daughter Denise with her, because her enthusiasm for life ended with his passing.

"I invited her to spend some time with me in California and she was the only person in the world I have ever trusted enough to discuss my unhappy marriage to Al Jolson. She never betrayed my confidence, but of course I knew she never would."

Up She Goes looked as though it would run forever and lasted a huge 256 performances.

"I went over to see Donny's show the day after my musical closed," said Virginia O'Brien. "He introduced me to Lawrence Anhalt who was about to produce *Princess Ida*, a musical by Sir Arthur Sullivan and W.S. Gilbert. Of course I had seen earlier brilliant Gilbert and Sullivan light operas and when Larry Anhalt offered me a principal role I jumped at the chance.

"Unhappily it was not one of Gilbert and Sullivan's best works and we closed after forty performances. By the end, the theatre was almost empty."

While *Up She Goes* was still running, Donald Brian accepted the lead in *Barnum Was Right*, a comedy drama. It was the first time he had worked in a show without dancing or singing, but the offer from John Meehan, one of the writers, to give him the lead intrigued him.

"I had often wondered how I would fare without my dancing shoes and with no songs to sing," he said in 1943.

Barnum Was Right opened in New York at the Frazee Theatre on March 12, 1923. It was originally expected to run for about six weeks, an acceptable time for a non-musical at that time, but the theatre was filled every night and producer Louis Werba convinced Donald Brian and the entire cast to extend the run to fourteen weeks.

15 Enter William Morris

Donald Brian told Walter Winchell that he missed the magic of a good musical, and when a member of the *Barnum Was Right* cast approached him to consider making a twelve-month tour to every major city outside New York with a revival of *No, No, Nanette*, a very successful musical a year or two earlier on Broadway, he jumped at the chance, but he said he would only accept if the other lead role went to Virginia.

"The actor who approached me about the tour was named William Morris. He had been considering for a while abandoning his acting career and concentrating his complete time and talents to a theatrical agency he had opened as a part time project a few years earlier. The William Morris Agency was later to become the largest and most successful theatrical agency in the world with offices in the United States, Canada, England and Australia.

"I was so impressed with the deal he got for both of us with *No, No, Nanette*," said Brian, "and when he suggested both Virginia and I had reached a time in our careers that we should concentrate on performing, leaving the financial negotiating to someone else, Virginia and I became the first major clients of the William Morris Agency.

"With our names on his books, he was soon able to sign some of the other top performers in New York for his agency. Letting him handle all our contracts was the best move either of us made in our careers. He may not have been a great actor, but he was a highly talented negotiator and when he told us what a management was offering we accepted because we knew it was the best deal possible.

"It was William Morris who suggested that we put away a quarter of all our earnings into investments and even suggested places to invest, including buildings and land in New York City, that made us a lot of money. He also put on one side enough to pay all our taxes, and he hired an accountant to see we got the best deal possible when tax time came around. We stayed with the agency for the rest of our careers, long enough to see his equally talented son, William Morris, Jr. take over the company.

"It was 1925 when we began our tour with *No, No, Nanette* and I was fifty years old. Virginia, with whom I had kept in close touch, was twenty-three. While we were on the road we were very close, spending most of our days exploring the treasures of the different cities we visited.

"Finally, on my fifty-first birthday, February 15, 1926, I knew it was now or never. Walking home from the theatre in Washington, the last stop on our tour, a day after we had dined with President Calvin Coolidge at the White House, I gambled my life on asking the question.

'Will you marry me Virginia,' I said. She stopped in her tracks, looked at me and said..."

Virginia O'Brien interrupted him. "I'll tell you exactly what I said. The words are engraved in my heart. I said, 'Donny, I would have married you when I was thirteen and I've waited ten years to hear those words. Yes, I'll marry you and I'll be your partner for life and I expect that to be a very long and happy life.' And it certainly has been, every day."

On their return to New York one week later, Donald Brian and Virginia O'Brien were married quietly at a Roman Catholic Church on Long Island. Only close friends were invited, and crowds of onlookers or flashing cameras from newsmen did not spoil the happiness of their wedding.

Walter Winchell was the first to hear about the marriage.

"What should have been the wedding of the year in New York took place quietly on Long Island last Saturday. Donald Brian and Virginia O'Brien were wed in a quiet ceremony that was uninterrupted by fans and newsmen. I congratulate them on getting married; it has been a long time coming for two people so obviously in love, and two people who are unquestionably the two nicest people in the entire world of entertainment.

"I understand that President Calvin Coolidge invited them to the White House in Washington when they visited the capital recently with *No, No, Nanette*. The invitation, I am told, was addressed to Mr. and Mrs. Donald Brian.

"I only hope President Coolidge is as intuitive in his matters of state as he was with this perceptive invitation."

16 Home Again

A week before their wedding Donald Brian asked Virginia if she would like to see the home in which he was born, in St. John's, Newfoundland. "I believe it will make a honeymoon never to be forgotten," he said.

"I learned later," she said in 1943, "that he had anticipated my saying 'yes' and had, through a friend, arranged for two rooms to be converted into a suite on a fishing trawler which regularly travelled from Boston to St. John's. We drove from New York to Boston to board the ship.

"At first glance the vessel didn't look too inviting, but when I saw the beautiful suite that had been made by knocking two cabins into one, I could never have asked for anything better. We ate quite wonderful meals prepared by a Boston chef, Cecil Lafarge, who Donny had hired to travel with us to ensure we got only the best food available. I remember one member of the crew telling me he had never before had meals like those prepared by Lafarge. 'I wish the skipper could afford him all the time,' he said.

"St. John's was everything Donny had said. It was stimulating and moving to see him wander around the town spotting places he knew.

"The only sad moment was when we visited a cemetery beside a Catholic Church to see the graves of the two men who started his career, Dennis Ryan and Herbert O'Sullivan. He explained that there was no grave for Billy Ryan, his first dance partner, because Billy had been lost at sea when his ship was sunk during the 1914-1918 war.

"Sadly he was unable to find his father's grave, and although they tried, nobody in the church was able to help him locate it.

"I was as sorry as he was to leave St. John's. But we will never go back again now, Donny is afraid too many things will have changed."

"It was the way it was when I was a child that I loved so much," he said.

On their return to New York Donald Brian gave an extra surprise to his new wife. He produced two tickets for the best suite on board the Cunard Lines flagship, the *S.S. Mauritania*, to England. At that time, the liner held the record, six days, for the fastest trip between New York and Southampton, England.

"I was so excited I could have jumped over the moon," said Virginia.

"We were away from home for just over four months. In England, Scotland, Ireland and Wales we travelled in a chauffeur driven car to all the places that were worth seeing.

"We saw Loch Ness, but no monster; we sat on the beautiful beach at Blackpool and ate delicious ice creams while we watched happy children at play; we saw ten musicals and dramas in London's West End and provincial theatres; we gazed at Buckingham Palace, but didn't see the king; we went half-way up Mount Snowden, with Donny dancing every inch of the climb; we renewed our wedding vows at Gretna Green, the famed village on the border of Scotland where English runaways had often been secretly married in a blacksmith's shop where such marriages were legal; we cruised along the River Thames; but above all we made many new friends who just knew us as ordinary people and liked us for what we were, not who we were."

"Perhaps that was the most wonderful thing about the trip," said Donny. "Nobody knew us. We were treated like ordinary people. Nobody was asking for autographs. Not one person asked us to do a dance for them."

"It really was Paradise," said Virginia. "The British people were kind and warm."

When they returned to New York, a *New York Times* photographer and reporter met them at the boat.

"We couldn't understand why they were there until the reporter asked, 'What date is the baby due,' Mrs. Brian.

Home Again

"Donny's jaw dropped open," said Virginia. "We both wondered how they could possibly have known the news that we had received in London only a day before sailing home again on the *Mauritania*."

It was many months later that they discovered a *New York Times* reporter working in London, who had seen them onstage in New York, spotted them entering the consulting office of a prominent Harley Street, London, gynaecologist and put two and two together.

The reporter sent a cable to Alexander Woollcott, by then a very successful New York writer, suggesting that he might get another scoop if the reporter's guess was right. Woollcott notified the editor and once again the *Times* did beat all the other papers with the news.

The Brians' daughter, Denise, arrived at eleven minutes after midnight on April 4, 1929.

"She was the one final thing we needed to make our lives complete," he said. "We gave her all the love we could, and she has repaid us a thousand times over by growing up to be the kind of daughter every family dreams about having.

"We had bought a lovely home in Great Neck, only a short car ride from New York, far enough to be away from the city, near enough to be ready to accept any shows the impresarios wanted to offer us."

While they were away in Europe, the Brians' financial adviser had sold most of their stocks and shares to provide the money to buy land on Long Island, which was fast becoming the "in-place" for New Yorkers fed up with the growing traffic and crowds in the city.

"When we returned home we were rather unhappy with some of the decisions he had made, but we had given him power of attorney and he had not broken any laws. A few months later we were thanking him for his judicious decisions."

In November 1929, the Brians had good reason to be grateful to their financial advisor. It was the month the New York Stock Exchange crashed.

"He called us in early November and told us that with only one exception he had taken us out of the New York Stock Exchange in time and that while values of the land he had purchased might drop temporarily, he was convinced that our capital losses would be very minor in the crash that made many millionaires into paupers overnight. He was right."

Offers from Broadway continued to pour in. On October 4, 1929, Donald Brian opened in a revival of an old comedy, *Becky Sharp*, at the Knickerbocker Theatre. "I had wanted to try another straight play," he told the *New York Post*. "*Becky Sharp* had been a success in 1895 and in two revivals in 1904 and 1917. When William Morris said the Players Club was considering bringing it back for another run, I urged that he try to get me the wonderful lead role of George Osborne. I was actually fifty-four at this stage in my career, but though I say it myself, I could easily be accepted as thirty-four.

"If writers didn't delve too deeply into my career and realise I had been on the New York stage for almost twenty-five years, I thought I could get away with it.

"Perhaps I should have listened to William Morris who was rather wary of the play. He feared it was too big a production to make a profit.

"The show, with a huge cast of fifty, rarely seen in a non-musical, had been adapted by Langdon Mitchell from *Vanity Fair* by William Makepeace Thackeray, to be appropriate for audiences in 1929, but it was not the success I had hoped and closed after only eighteen performances.

"It was obvious even during rehearsals that a comedy with such a large cast would have to do capacity business to pay its way. We got good reviews, but the crowds didn't come in large enough numbers to make the show profitable.

"Before *Becky Sharp* closed I had already been approached by William Morris to star in another non-musical, *Here's Your Health* planned for the Vanderbilt Theatre. It had a perfect role for Virginia and since we had found a wonderful nanny, Ethel Lucas, to look after Denise at night, she agreed to take it, saying that it would likely be her final stage appearance."

Once again the show failed to draw crowds. Unemployment had skyrocketed following the stock market crash and New Yorkers had little money to spare for nights out on the town. Late in January 1930, producer Lyle Andrews decided to close it down.

"Virginia and I were now happy to stay home with Denise," said Brian in 1943, "Thanks to our financial advisor's solid investments in property, we had enough money to keep us for the rest of our lives, even if neither of us ever worked again.

"It was in 1930 that for the first time in my entire career that I began to wonder if my approach to performance, acting, singing and dancing had finally gone out of style."

William Morris again came to the rescue. He told the *New York Times* in 1931 that Donald Brian had probably danced and sung in New York for the last time.

"But Mr. Brian is receiving a lot of interest from producers in Hollywood who realise, with sound films becoming the rage, his great experience as a stage actor will make him very valuable to directors in need of actors with know-how and voices that will record well."

Making arrangements to close down their Great Neck home for an indefinite time, the Brians hired a gardener and a housekeeper. Ethel Lucas had agreed to go with them to Hollywood, and she and Denise went along on a cross-country trip that turned out to be much longer than any of them had anticipated. Just before they were due to leave New York, a startling new offer came along from William Morris.

"How would you like to play Prince Danilo in *The Merry Widow* one last time?" asked Milton Aborn, a director with the New York Civic Light Opera Company.

"I told him, at fifty-six, I couldn't imagine any very beautiful merry widow falling in love with me at my age," he said.

Milton Aborn had the perfect answer. "If Sonia, the Merry Widow, was played by your wife, Virginia O'Brien, would that help convince you to take the role?"

Donald Brian was intrigued. Virginia told him he could still pass for thirty and she urged him to accept the role.

"But it was ten days before I had summoned up the courage to accept," Donald Brian told the *Los Angeles Examiner* in 1934.

"How could I argue with Virginia playing the role of Sonia. We were scheduled to play for only three weeks starting in January of 1931 at Erlanger's Theatre in New York before going on a cross-country tour of twelve weeks that would end in Los Angeles.

"When we were preparing for *The Merry Widow*, Virginia and I had an odd experience one night walking back to the hotel where we stayed when rehearsals went late into the night. The night was warm and we had decided to walk. Suddenly a complete stranger slapped me on the back. I had become used to exuberant fans so just smiled and tried to walk away. But the stranger blocked my path.

'Mr. Brian,' he said. 'I have enjoyed many of your musical shows, I shall hope to see *The Merry Widow* when it reaches Washington.'

'Is that your home sir,' I said.

'Indeed, yes,' said the stranger.

'I don't believe I know you, sir?' I said

'You should Mr. Brian, I'm your president.'

"I was shocked and embarrassed to realise it was President Herbert Hoover! He shook my hand, laughed, and walked away into the night. He was the sixth president I had met, but surely that meeting was the most unceremonious."

Every seat in Erlanger's Theatre was sold for the three-week run in New York of *The Merry Widow* and on the final night, flowers handed up from the audience almost covered the stage. After the opening night, the *New York Times* was very generous. The headline on the review read:

King Of Broadway Crowned Again
By A Most Delectable Merry Widow

"The review was kind and even if most of our audience was made up of people in their fifties and above, their enthusiasm was infectious and I even dared to try out a few steps from the 1907 production that had Virginia believing I had been reincarnated.

"For the cross-country tour the company was given four private first class coaches and two baggage vans for the scenery and costumes."

"We had kitchens and a chef on board so we could eat any time we wished," said Virginia. "There was a private room for Donny and I, if we needed to rest. Another room was allocated to Denise and Ethel. It was a luxurious way to travel. All the journeys were on Sundays so we arrived in each new city in time to check into the beautiful suites reserved for us in the best hotels."

"The entire cast, including stage and lighting crew members, were housed in the same first class hotels," said Donald Brian. "In all my time as an entertainer, I could never recall being treated so grandly as we were on that exciting and memorable journey from coast-to-coast.

"On two occasions, when there was no convenient train to which we could have our cars attached, a special engine was attached to our coaches and we were taken to the next town, as a complete train, in time for us to rest before the Monday opening. It was a time in our lives we shall never forget. We both wished that Denise, then nearly three, had been old enough to enjoy the luxury of that journey and the magnificent scenery that thrilled us every leg of the way.

"On the tour we played Boston, Washington, Buffalo, Chicago, St. Louis, New Orleans, Dallas, Houston, San Francisco, and before we knew it we were in Los Angeles. We filled every theatre along the way and received standing ovations each night. It was perhaps the most memorable time for Virginia and I in our entire careers," said Brian.

"Virginia and I had, of course, met President Hoover rather unexpectedly on a New York street, and in Washington we received an unexpected invitation from him. He requested the presence of the entire cast of *The Merry Widow* at a luncheon at the White House. He also invited many of Washington's top politicians to the banquet and after the meal, all the young ladies from the show were dancing around with elderly, and previous rather pompous, members of the government. It was only after the evening was over that I realized President Hoover had invited none of the wives of these prominent politicians, so none were there to see the rather wild behaviour of their husbands.

"President Hoover whispered to me, 'I wish I could get them so eager to please when I present bills in the house, but I fear your dancers have much more appeal than me. I have a tough week in the house ahead, so perhaps you could lend me a few of your young dancers.'

"I didn't know if he was serious, so I just smiled and said nothing.

"President Hoover was seated in a private box on the third night of our stay in Washington. At the final curtain, he stood and cheered with the audience."

17 Hollywood Welcome

"In Los Angeles, where we stayed three weeks, all the friends I had made in the theatre who were then in Hollywood were out front and we had a party after the show almost every night.

"I spotted W.C. Fields in the stage box on opening night. During the performance he kept rather loudly singing the songs in the show with us. His voice was not altogether musical, but it was not until I finally went to the side of the stage near his box and told him I would like him to come onstage to do a dance with Virginia that he quieted down and sat back to enjoy the show.

"He had said nothing to Virginia or I, but after the show we found a limousine at the stage door waiting to take us to a party at the Hollywood Hotel on Hollywood Boulevard. There we met many of Fields' friends in the film industry. Although few, if any, had appeared on Broadway, they seemed to know who we were and gave us a great ovation when we arrived at the hotel.

"I particularly remember Mae West. Her reputation as an actress and other things had, by that time, spread worldwide. She took Virginia on one side and offered her $10,000 if she would let her take over the role of Sonia in the show for one performance.

"Virginia thought very fast, not wanting to hurt this rather charming lady, and said perhaps if she would stand on the side of the stage each night watching the show she might be ready to take over the role at the Monday night performance two weeks ahead.

"Mae West attended every show and was actually very graceful trying out the steps. On the Saturday night before her 'debut' we had to 'very regretfully' tell her that the management had decided to close the show immediately and there would be no Monday performance.

"Mae laughed loudly. 'You think I didn't know,' she said. 'I couldn't have cared a damn about the role, all I wanted was to stand side stage each night to see you, Donny, dancing around in those skin tight trousers. I hoped one night they might have split, but they didn't.'

"She shook hands with us and had this parting comment: 'You won't, of course, get the $10,000, but if Donny's pants had split just once I would have given you the money anyway.'"

Louis B. Mayer, head of Metro-Goldwyn-Mayer studios attended the show one evening. After the final curtain, he went around backstage to speak to Donald Brian.

'I am just about ready to produce a film version of *The Merry Widow*,' he said. 'I have the cast completed, but had I known how good you were I would have been willing to offer you the role you are playing tonight in the film.'

"I told Mr. Mayer that at my age it would be foolish to consider playing any roles in films that were not character roles," said Brian.

'If that is what you want, Mr. Brian, please come to my studio tomorrow and I will have a $2,000 a week contract for eight weeks waiting on my desk. I will have my car at the Biltmore Hotel at 10:00 in the morning. You may have your pick of the roles my producers will offer and you may turn down any you dislike.

'After that eight weeks, I will hire you for five more weeks at $5,000 a week to act as choreography supervisor during the making of *The Merry Widow*. You will have the power to veto anything you see that is out of keeping with the great tradition of this wonderful musical.

'I have told the director, Ernst Lubitsch, that he is to agree to anything you suggest. And whenever possible, in the ballroom scenes, I hope your good wife, Virginia and you will dance around the floor for the cameras. Virginia will receive $2,000 for each week of production. You can either be credited on the screen for this work or not, as you wish, but I feel your presence on the set will help enhance the standard of everyone's work.

Hollywood Welcome

'One final thing, Mr. Brian, tomorrow at your matinee performance you will have the most star-studded audience before which any performer has ever played. I have bought out the entire theatre and the cast of *The Merry Widow* at MGM will be in the front seats, other actors from MGM and many of our top technicians will fill the rest of the theatre.'

"I was so stunned I could hardly answer," said Brian. "I thanked Mr. Mayer, told him I would gladly accept, and waited to see who was in the audience at the matinee next day.

"The MGM *Merry Widow* cast was one of the most glamorous ever assembled in Hollywood. In the audience were Maurice Chevalier, Jeanette MacDonald, Edward Everett Horton, Una Merkel, Minna Gombell, Ruth Channing, Sterling Holloway, Henry Armetta, Donald Meek, Akim Tamiroff, Herman Bing, and the film's director Ernst Lubitsch.

"In addition there were other MGM stars including Bette Davis, Stan Laurel and Oliver Hardy, Lionel Barrymore, Nelson Eddy, Myrna Loy, Charles Laughton, Warner Oland, Ned Sparks, and William Powell. The wonderful Marie Dressler, who had helped me organize a parade of the underpaid chorus dancers on Broadway more than twenty years earlier, sent a handwritten note with Mr. Mayer. It said she regretted not being present since she was rather unwell. Sadly, she died only one week later before I had a chance to see her again."

After the show, Mayer lined all his stars onstage together with director Ernst Lubitsch, and introduced them one by one to Donald Brian and Virginia O'Brien.

"I couldn't help thinking of a clever dog act I once saw in a circus," said Brian. "If only Mr. Mayer had brandished a whip, he would have been just like the dog trainer lining up his animals for their ultimate trick."

The final introduction was to Ernst Lubitsch, renowned as being an independent director who hated outside interference.

"I had been told that Lubitsch was a difficult man to work with," said Brian in 1943, "so I drew him to one side. 'Mr. Lubitsch,' I said. 'I have no plans to interfere with your work. You alone will have the final say in your decision to approve or veto any suggestions I may make. I will gladly bow to your superior knowledge of directing a film.'

"Lubitsch looked at me, and a rare smile broke out on his face.

'Mr. Brian,' he said, 'and I promise I will bow to your superior knowledge of dancing.'

"We never had a cross word on the set and he and I often had lunch together in the studio commissary. Throughout the five weeks of filming, the only tantrums came not from Lubitsch, but [from] Maurice Chevalier who got very temperamental at times. I recall being amazed that the wonderful French accent he used onscreen didn't exist off the set. Unless there were newspaper people present who might have revealed his secret, he spoke perfect English with hardly a trace of a French accent.

"Louis B. Mayer came to me on the final day of shooting and shook my hand. He said, 'It would be a great waste of your abilities as an actor or I would hire you to be on the MGM staff exclusively to help keep the peace on every Lubitsch film.'"

The Merry Widow from MGM was a huge success at the box-office and is available today on video. If you look closely you will be able to spot Donald Brian and Virginia O'Brien dancing with the other extras in two scenes. And a few close-ups of dancing feet are not those of Chevalier and MacDonald, they are those of Donald and Virginia Brian. But neither of the Brians is named in the credits.

The film was one of the largest grossing MGM films of the year.

Mayer wanted to put Donald Brian on long-term contract, but he declined. Virginia had earlier turned a similar offer down. "I don't think I will ever act again," she said. "My life now will be devoted to looking after my husband and our daughter Denise."

18 On Broadway Again

While still wondering whether it was time to retire or whether his future lay in the character roles he was enjoying playing in Hollywood, Donald Brian received a phone call from William Morris in New York. That call put both he and Virginia back to work in a most unexpected place – on Broadway in New York.

'I have a lucrative offer for you to produce and direct a new version of *The Chocolate Soldier* that will open at the St. James Theatre in New York in May of this year,' said Morris. 'In addition George M. Cohan has asked me to plead with you to appear with Virginia as stars of his latest musical comedy, *The Song and Dance Man*. He wants to open it later this year. The salary and percentage George M. is offering is more than anyone else is receiving now on Broadway.

'He wants you back in New York, I want you back in New York, how about you?' he said.

"Working at MGM was an easy life. In the weeks before *The Merry Widow* film I had played rather enjoyable, but small roles in more than ten films. Used to working six days each week on Broadway, I was at times rather bored. I suddenly realised that although the weather was great, I could put up with the winter of New York, if I could once again hear the applause of the audience at the end of each performance.

"I said 'yes' to William Morris and 'no' to offers from Hollywood. Our caretaker and housekeeper were given instructions to ready our Great Neck house for our arrival and Virginia and I, together with Denise and Ethel, booked a complete private coach on the fastest train back to New York City.

"Sid Olcott offered to find a tenant for our Beverly Hills house on a monthly basis, so that if we wanted to come back he could have the home waiting for us. Before we left, he confirmed that Charles Laughton and his wife Elsa Lanchester, with whom we had become very friendly, had seen the house and loved it.

'They will move out of their hotel immediately,' he said, 'They promise to take care of your furniture and other possessions while they are there.'

The Chocolate Soldier was not the big success everyone hoped at the St. James Theatre.

"Charles Purcell, who held the production rights, refused to accept the fact that the show that was such a hit twenty years earlier was terribly outdated in 1934," said Donald Brian. "Happily I was not onstage and felt badly for Mr. Purcell who had cast himself in the role of Lieutenant Bumerli that I had last played in 1926. He hired his girlfriend, Bernice Claire, to play Nadia, the principal female role, and she just didn't have the strength to make the role believable.

"Purcell had previously staged *The Chocolate Soldier* several years earlier, but the show then only lasted twenty-eight performances. This version, with Bernice Claire, whose only previous experience was in vaudeville, was doomed to failure from the opening night.

"I was embarrassed that the audience, many of whom had expected from the rather fraudulent publicity Charles Purcell had handed out to the newspapers and radio stations that I would be onstage, and at the final curtain they were calling my name. I finally walked onstage and took a bow. I left the theatre that night knowing the show would not run for long. It survived only thirteen nights."

Virginia O'Brien added this comment. "Donny will never tell you this secret, but I will. He handed his entire fee back to Mr. Purcell because he felt sorry for him and the large financial loss Purcell must have suffered with the production."

But George M. Cohan's *Song and Dance Man* was a very different story. "It was written as the story of a song and dance man who just couldn't give up the spotlight. It had superb musical numbers, and if the audience finally accepted that I was no longer young it didn't matter. George M. had written my musical swan song to perfection," said Donald Brian.

On Broadway Again

On the opening night at the final curtain, the orchestra struck up the music of *Give My Regards to Broadway*.

"I was stunned, didn't really know what to do until George M. walked onstage and started tap dancing. I joined him and we did a routine we hadn't done in twenty years, but the audience loved it. It was so successful that George M. was there every night and we did our song and dance routine at every one of the 120 shows that drew capacity audiences to the theatre every night.

"When the final curtain came down early in 1935, on my sixtieth birthday, I knew I was enjoying being old for the first time in my life."

In his memoirs George M. Cohan said this of *The Song and Dance Man*: "What Donny didn't realise," he wrote, "is that the show was my swan song as much as his. I found it hard to get out of the spotlight and let Donny tell the story for me."

In the cast of the musical were two young actors just starting their climb to the top.

"I told Louis B. Mayer, who was in New York for a few days, that these two young actors were surely going to be stars. He came to see our show and two days later he had signed both Humphrey Bogart and Broderick Crawford to MGM contracts to start immediately following their run in *The Song and Dance Man*. Both, as everyone knows, became very successful in Hollywood. Broderick is of course now (1943) in the U.S. Army and is shortly to go over to Europe with Captain Glenn Miller and his Orchestra."

Walter Winchell officially announced Donald Brian's retirement as a dancer with these words:

> "A long and illustrious career has come to an end with the final curtain of *The Song and Dance Man*. Donald Brian has left the stage with dignity and charm. He feels he is now too old to continue dancing and singing, and while I don't agree with that decision I applaud his intelligence in getting out of a rapidly changing musical theatre in New York while he is still the King Of Broadway.

Donald Brian: The King of Broadway

> "What will Donald Brian do now? He and his wife are retiring to their lovely home in Great Neck to devote their time and talents to their twelve year old daughter, Denise, the kind of life that few other children will ever be fortunate enough to experience.
>
> "You have not been dethroned Donald Brian, you have simply abdicated your throne to others who will have grave difficulty in their attempts to emulate your brilliance as an actor, dancer, singer and gentleman."

Eight months later Walter Winchell was again the first to mention in his column that Donald Brian was no longer retired and would star in 1935 at the Forty-Eighth Street Theatre in Dorothy Bennett and Irving White's new comedy, *Fly Away Home*.

"I am delighted to see him back and even more delighted to see that he will stress his inimitable talents not in singing and dancing, but in comedy.

"I have not yet attended a rehearsal, but can without doubt predict that *Fly Away Home* will be one of the shows to see this year on Broadway."

Fly Away Home was indeed a witty comedy that the critics loved. Donald Brian was once again a star on Broadway.

"I love the role and am finding that clever humour provided by Dorothy Bennett and Irving White is my forte. I can return home every night and appearing in this wonderful play is making my life complete," he told the *New York Times*.

Again Donald Brian used his influence with Louis B. Mayer to get a Hollywood contract for a young actor who had, until *Fly Away Home*, not had a part good enough on Broadway to attract the attention of critics.

Montgomery Clift told the *Hollywood Reporter* in 1942 that he was just about ready to abandon his hopes in the world of show business until "Donald Brian offered me the role of Harman Masters in *Fly Away Home*. He was not officially the play's director, but both he and his wife, Virginia, spent hours with me perfecting my role.

On Broadway Again

"I knew it had not been in vain when I received my first standing ovation at the final curtain on the opening night of the play. The play was actually staged by Thomas Mitchell who already had a distinguished career as an actor, director and playwright. As most people know, he too went to Hollywood at the urging of Donald Brian and has been a huge success on the screen in character roles.

"Mr. Mitchell was so enamoured of Donald Brian's work on the play that he convinced the producer, Thomas Bamberger, to list him on the program not as director, but with these words, 'Staged by Thomas Mitchell.' I learned at the end of the play's run that Donald Brian refused to be named director saying, 'I only assisted the talented Mr. Mitchell.'"

19 Return to Hollywood

Just before *Fly Away Home* closed after 136 performances, Donald and Virginia Brian received a call from Sid Olcott in Hollywood.

"I told them that Charles Laughton was returning to England for at least a year to make films over there," he said, "and that their house on Bedford Drive would be empty early in March. I told him there were lots of British actors in Hollywood at that time looking for houses to rent in Beverly Hills. I asked if they wanted me to make inquiries and find a new tenant. Donny surprised me with his immediate response.

"He said no to both suggestions because he was bringing his family back to Hollywood in April as the William Morris office in Los Angeles had received so many offers of character roles from different film studios."

Donald Brian remembered that decision in 1943: "I sensed there would be no more Broadway shows for a sixty year old, but was constantly hearing from Louis B. Mayer that he had roles in a dozen or more films that would be ideal for me."

Louis B. Mayer was very honest. "They won't be starring roles," he said, "but they will be character roles you can get your teeth into and will enjoy doing. How soon can we expect you back?"

Donald Brian, who had already thought seriously about a possible move to California, had received approval in advance from both Virginia and Denise. Ethel Lucas, still with the family as a companion for Denise, said she would also be happy to make the move.

"So it was easy for me to tell Sid Olcott that we were coming, and a phone call to Louie Mayer confirmed that work would be waiting."

Between 1936 and 1939 Donald Brian appeared in more than forty films at MGM, Warner Brothers, Universal and Paramount. Many of the people he had given encouragement in New York, now stars in their own right, were anxious to work with him again.

"When we arrived in Hollywood, I took over my old home again. Charles Laughton had left it in immaculate condition and he even left the names and phone numbers of efficient house staff he had employed," said Brian.

"On my first night back in our old home I had to run to the front window to see what was going on outside. A brass band was blaring out the *Merry Widow Waltz*. Conducting was my old friend, W.C. Fields. He saw Virginia and I looking out of the window and beckoned to us. We went outside to find a gaudily decorated convertible car waiting. A man standing by our front door told us to climb aboard.

"Fields then led the parade down Bedford Drive to Sunset Boulevard and on to the Beverly Hills Hotel. I didn't realise he was fit enough to walk that distance. At the hotel every performer I had worked with in New York was waiting for us in the ballroom.

"W.C. Fields had hired Johnny Green and his orchestra. The *Merry Widow Waltz* was playing as we entered and Virginia and I had to lead the dancers around the floor while those who couldn't dance applauded. I had made a record with Johnny and his Orchestra almost twenty years earlier while I was appearing on Broadway in *The Girl from Utah*. The song *Gilbert the Filbert* was the hit song of the show, but so far as I know the record never became a bestseller.

"Fortunately in those days, even at home without planning to go out anywhere, men and women dressed immaculately and so we were not out of place in the midst of all this glamour.

"Johnny Green and his orchestra played every song from every musical in which I had ever appeared and the finale came when Johnny invited me onstage to sing a couple of choruses of *Give My Regards to Broadway*.

"When we were all danced out, we were directed into a private dining room for a mouth-watering banquet. A great big 'Welcome Home Donny and Virginia' sign covered one wall. I had to make a speech and I think they applauded every sentence.

"There were more than a hundred people present, including Louis B. Mayer and Jack Warner. I noticed two cameramen filming much of the dancing and the microphone on the head table at the banquet was not there to amplify my voice, but for the sound engineer to add sound to the film.

"The saddest thing about that glorious night is that I never did get to see the film. On the way home the camera and sound crew, who had unfortunately perhaps had a little too much to drink, were involved in a horrific crash that flipped their vehicle over. They got out alive, but the truck burst into flames, destroying a memory that I think I would be watching today if it still existed."

Donald Brian passed on every work offer he received to the Los Angeles office of the William Morris Agency.

"I could have worked seven days a week, but Virginia and I were busy showing Denise all the wonderful sights of California, so I just accepted one and two-day roles that allowed me to keep the rest of the week free.

"It was a glorious time in all our lives," he recalled in 1943. "Hollywood really was the paradise everyone believed it to be. We climbed in the hills, swam at the beach or just accepted the wonderful invitations we were receiving from some of the biggest names in Hollywood.

"Mary Pickford called Denise every morning when I was working or had other plans. If Denise wasn't busy Mary sent her chauffeur-driven limousine to our house to take Denise back to her showplace home, Pickfair, to swim in her pool with her other guests. I remember Denise coming home one day to tell me she had been playing tennis with Greta Garbo. I was jealous. I never did meet Garbo.

"Although I was really only a supporting character actor by this time, Hollywood's most important people treated us as if we were as important as them.

Return to Hollywood

"It never ceases to amaze me how many of Hollywood's biggest stars started their careers on the Broadway stage. Louie Mayer once told me that he always tried to hire actors with a stage background because the discipline they learned in the theatre made them ready to accept the direction they needed in the film industry."

20 One More Time in New York

At that stage in his career, Donald Brian never dreamed that he would ever return to Broadway. But he did.

In 1938 while working at Paramount Studios he was introduced to the prolific composer Jerome Kern.

"Mr. Brian," said Kern, "somebody just told me you are sixty-three years old. I find that impossible to believe and I would like to invite you back to Broadway not for a drama, but a musical comedy that Oscar Hammerstein and I have just completed.

"We have the theatre, the Alvin, the show, *Very Warm for May*, and an opening date of Friday, November 17. We have Oscar's wonderful book and lyrics and my music. I promise it will be the kind of music you love. We have a great director, young Vincente Minnelli, who has also designed the costumes and sets. I think we will hear a lot more from him in the years ahead. If you join us you will be joining a very illustrious cast including Jack Whiting, Eve Arden and Grace McDonald."

Jerome Kern was right; Vincente Minnelli went on to Hollywood after the New York production and directed many of MGM's greatest musicals. He was also the husband of Judy Garland and the father of Liza Minnelli.

"Most of the cast has been assembled right now for *Very Warm for May*," said Kern, "but until today neither Oscar nor I could think of anyone suitable to play the role of William Graham, a not-so-young owner of a lovely home at Great Neck, New York. I find it hard to believe you are middle aged, but I am told you actually own a home in Great Neck, so you would be right at home in our show.

"Can I invite you back to Broadway, Mr. Brian?"

"I asked for a few days to consider the offer, an opportunity to hear the music and read the script. But it only took me twenty-four hours before I said 'yes.'"

One More Time in New York

Once again the Brian family returned to their Great Neck home. "We kept the Bedford Drive home because we thought we might one day be returning to California. Sid Olcott found us a nice film couple from England, then working in Hollywood, and they took a month-by-month lease until we decided to return."

Very Warm for May, Jerome Kern's last Broadway musical, was not one of Kern and Hammerstein's biggest Broadway successes, but it ran for eighty-three performances in the early days of World War II that had begun in September.

"Although the United States was not yet in the war, the face of Broadway changed almost overnight," said Donald Brian. "Patriotic shows took over and the Broadway musicals, getting very expensive to stage with large casts, were getting fewer and fewer.

"When the show closed, I went home to Great Neck and devoted almost two years to my family. My working days were dedicated to helping the American Theatre Wing, which was becoming more and more important in ensuring the well-being of every performer appearing on Broadway. [It is the American Theatre Wing that today presents the annual TV show honouring Broadway's best, and distributes the Tony Awards.]

"Early in March 1942, with America then into World War II, the Theatre Wing decided to open a centre offering only the very top stars as entertainers and free food for as many servicemen and women visiting New York as possible.

"When the New York Stage Door Canteen opened its doors in the superbly renovated rehearsal room on 44th Street that I had once used for my dancing school, Virginia and I were asked to cut the ribbon for the official opening before giving an exhibition of dancing to the music of Tommy Dorsey and his Orchestra. Then we asked for servicemen and women who would like to dance with us. Virginia's first partner was a young soldier, Private Clyde Burns, who had danced in the chorus of several touring musicals. My first partner, Sergeant Monica Freeman, turned out to be a competent dancer who had worked in musical theatre in Chicago.

"Later that evening, we took Sgt. Freeman and Pte. Burns out for a late supper at Toots Shor's Restaurant, then the finest eatery in New York. We kept in touch for several years. Unhappily, Clyde Burns was killed in the invasion of Europe, but Monica Freeman married an English army captain and stayed in England when the war ended. Sadly we lost touch."

Donald and Virginia Brian spent many hours every day backstage at New York theatres and at the radio studios convincing as many entertainers as possible to entertain at the Stage Door Canteen.

"When we weren't wanted as entertainers, we put on aprons and helped serve the hot dogs, sandwiches and Coca-Cola the guests enjoyed."

In January 1942, *This is the Army*, a musical tribute to the United States Army, had opened on Broadway. Written by Irving Berlin, one of his songs *This is the Army, Mr. Jones,* quickly became a number one hit. Every cent the show and its music raised went to the Army Emergency Relief Fund. Berlin never took a cent for himself.

After his own show closed for the night, Irving Berlin walked over to the Stage Door Canteen on its opening night and sat down at the piano and played every one of his popular songs the service men and women present requested.

When the last person had left the canteen Berlin came over to Donny Brian who was helping wash the dishes. "Come and listen to this," he said, as he walked back to the piano. "We need a love song in *This is the Army*. I watched the servicemen here tonight falling in love with every one of the young dancers who made them forget for a minute that they were in a war." He sat at the piano and played the first eight bars of a song that is still memorable today, sixty-three years after it was written.

"Berlin sang the first two lines, '*I left my heart at the Stage Door Canteen. I left it there with a girl named Eileen.*'"

"That's all I've got so far Donny, but I'll finish it tonight and it will be in *This is the*

Army next week. Tomorrow, I'll bring you a copy of the lyrics and I want you to be the first to sing it right here in the Stage Door Canteen."

"He told me later that he finished the song in forty-five minutes after he reached his home," said Brian in 1943. "Irving Berlin is an incredible man who can't even read music."

As promised, Irving Berlin returned the next night with *I Left My Heart at the Stage Door Canteen*. He handed the lyrics to Donny and asked him to sing it. It was the first time the song was ever sung in public. As Berlin had predicted, it became the hit song in *This is the Army*, and before the end of 1942, it was the Number One hit of the year.

The Brians also made regular appearances on the Stage Door Canteen radio show which went on the air from the NBC New York studios every Thursday from 9:30 to 10:00 p.m. The show's resident orchestra leader, Raymond Paige, said the Brians were much more than just entertainers.

"We used NBC's 1,500-seat studio and filled it every Thursday with servicemen and women. We gave them a ninety-minute show before we went on the air. None of the entertainers got paid a cent, and since nobody was officially under contract, there were many nights when big names found it impossible to appear. A phone call to Donny and Virginia brought them to the studio as fill-ins and rarely did we have time to rehearse. We kept all their music at the studio and often handed it out to the band only minutes before the show was due to start. I remember one night when Judy Garland's manager called to say she was too ill to appear that Donny and Virginia did the entire pre-show and radio show themselves. Bert Lytell, our master-of-ceremonies crossed his fingers many nights, but always heaved a sign of relief when Donny and Virginia arrived at the studio.

"I don't believe any records were kept of the Brians' appearances, but without them the show could never have gone on, and thousands of servicemen and women would have been disappointed. I can't emphasize enough how generous they were and how easy to work with."

In 1945, when the war in Europe ended, the radio show ended and the Stage Door Canteen finally closed its doors.

Bert Lytell said this to the *New York Daily News*: "It wasn't easy to get the big stars we needed to keep the show going. They were probably given about ten dollars to help pay their taxi fares, but we knew in any emergency we could call Donald and Virginia Brian, usually to be found serving hot dogs at the Stage Door Canteen, and they would be here in less than ten minutes to get us out of a hole.

"Our sponsor, the Corn Products Refining Company, were so delighted with Donny and Virginia that every time they stepped in to keep the show going they sent a substantial cheque to the American Theatre Wing to help buy the ever-increasing amounts of food needed to keep the very successful Stage Door Canteen open."

21 Enter Bob Hope

In November 1942, the Brians returned to Hollywood. The Hollywood Canteen was scheduled to open as a west coast version of the New York Stage Door Canteen. They were asked to be the first performers, dancing to the music of Harry James and his Orchestra. "Often we were there five, six or even seven nights a week. Very few servicemen and women knew who we were, so most of the time we just served food and Coca-Cola to the guests," said Virginia. "Donny and I were not unhappy to be unknowns. It was something new for us and we liked it. But next year, that anonymity was to vanish."

In March 1943 the front door bell rang at the Brians' Bedford Drive home. The familiar face of Bob Hope greeted them at the door.

"We had met Bob Hope several times before," said Virginia. "First time was in 1939, when he was already a big star. Donny played a character role in a Paramount film, *Give Me A Sailor*, and we had seen a few of his early stage appearances in New York before Hollywood called him. And, of course, Bob was a regular entertainer at the Hollywood Canteen.

'Please come in,' we said in unison. 'Virginia and I stood aside to allow the great Paramount star to enter. We asked him to sit down and this is just about the exact never-to-be-forgotten conversation to which we listened.'

'Mr. and Mrs. Brian,' said Hope, 'I was an enthusiast of your work for many years before I came to Hollywood. Mr. Brian, you should know that I was once a nervous performer who sometimes had difficulty learning my lines because the thought of standing in front of an audience petrified me.

'I did get backstage when you were doing *The Chocolate Soldier* and I asked for your help. I told you my nervousness was not helping my career, and I asked you how you were able to be so relaxed onstage. You didn't know me from Adam, but you found time to help me when I was just beginning my career.

'You told me your secret, that you concentrated on just one person in the audience, a smiling person, and delivered all your lines to him or her. You suggested I do the same.

'I did what you said, always choosing a beautiful girl who I hoped would later come backstage to meet me. Rapidly I was a different performer. Within a month I was being offered better roles on Broadway and then out of the blue came a contract from Hollywood.

'I must also tell you that my meagre dancing skills all came from watching you and now I want to ask you one more favour. Will you come with me and a troupe of performers who are going over to England to entertain not only the American troops over there, but any other troops we can find who know enough English to appreciate my humour? You may not know, Mr. Brian, but I was born in England and have a very soft spot in my heart for the old country. I know you come from Newfoundland and that too really is part of England.

'We would do a dance routine together, you adding more and more tricky steps as we went along and I would try to copy, but more often than not end on my rear end. The service men and women love to see me being beaten by a better man.

'I need you, Mr. Brian, to be that better man. There won't be any money in it, but we will get a little closer to the war and to those men and women about to go into battle.

'We may have to work out of doors on temporary stages at some camps, and I should warn you that it rains a lot in England, but we never cancel a show.

'We will fly in military planes to New York, then directly over to London. Often we will sleep in cots on the bases at which we entertain. It won't be glamorous, but I promise you it will be memorable.

'One thing more, before we go, I will need you to teach me a few of your dance steps so I won't look too much of a fool. Do we have a deal?'

"Tears were running down Donny's cheeks," recalled Virginia. "But I heard him say that he would be ready whenever Bob Hope was.

'Then you and I had better rent a rehearsal studio today so you can teach me to be a much better dancer than I am now. We will both be measured and kitted out with U.S. Army uniforms and then we'll meet with the rest of the unit and work out the complete show.

'One thing more, since we will mostly be performing before U.S. soldiers thousands of miles from home, I shall want you to sing while I dance to *Give My Regards to Broadway*. It will be the finale and I guarantee a showstopper.'

"I jumped up and hugged Bob Hope," said Virginia. "I told him, 'You have just taken twenty years off our lives.'

"Without a trace of a smile Bob Hope responded instantly. "Then I'll put Donny down on the cast list as being just sixteen.'

Bob Hope recalls that trip to England in one of his many autobiographies.

"I have never worked with a more unassuming performer than Donald Brian. I learned during the flight over that he was sixty-eight, but he passed for forty everywhere we played, and his energy was more like a twenty year old.

"He could change routines on the spot if I saw something going over well and wanted to keep the skit or dance going.

"Some of the company were quite scared at the thought of going to Britain's south coast and into the bases near London which were being bombed regularly. But Donny had a wonderful knack of making every situation into an enjoyable one. He calmed fears with that wonderful style that had made him a big star on Broadway twenty or thirty years earlier.

"At one base we were told General Eisenhower would be in the audience, and before the show the general asked not for me but Donny to visit his quarters.

"When Donny returned he looked amazed. This is what he told us."

'General Eisenhower shook hands and said he was delighted to see me,' he said. 'Not only myself but many of our officers are old enough to remember you on Broadway and I want you to know that if you hear a special burst of applause tonight it will be from me and my senior officers.'"

When the show returned from England, Bob Hope and the entire troupe were invited to visit President Franklin D. Roosevelt in the White House.

"Once again," he said in 1943, "I met another president of the United States, my seventh. I admired President Roosevelt for his courage to beat the paralysis that kept him for years in a wheelchair. When I told him this, he laughed.

'I think you had more courage than me when you appeared in *Becky Sharp* on Broadway in 1929,' he said. 'Eleanor and I had previously seen you in *Buddies* and *Up She Goes*, very successful musicals, but *Becky Sharp*? How did you ever get convinced to star in that out of date bomb? That was more courageous than anything I ever will ever do.'"

In meeting General Eisenhower in England, Donald Brian was actually meeting his eighth president, although nobody at that time had ever considered the general as a future president.

22 Frank Sinatra

Before returning to Hollywood, Donald Brian took a train from Washington to New York where he had reserved a suite at the Waldorf Astoria Hotel.

"It was a hopeful move because I actually thought perhaps William Morris might astonish me and make me an offer I couldn't refuse. But he didn't, and after two weeks of waiting I was disillusioned for the first time in my life and was ready to pack my bags to head back to Hollywood. Then, the telephone rang!

"The call I received was totally unexpected. It was from a young singer who had just left the Tommy Dorsey Orchestra and had set out in the world as a solo performer. He had a radio show, *Your Hit Parade*, and was making personal appearances at the biggest theatres to huge audiences.

'Mr. Brian,' said Frank Sinatra, 'I need your help. When I was with Tommy Dorsey all I had to do was clutch a microphone and sing. Now I am expected to move around the stage and I feel very uncomfortable making any moves. I'm told you are the most relaxed person in show business and are so graceful that everyone loves every move you make. I need you to help me to find that secret of relaxation and even more important how to move on the stage. I need you desperately before I destroy my career,' said Sinatra.

"We met that same day," recalled Brian. "It was easy to see he was tense and had needed to be shown how to loosen up. I told him the same tale I had told W.C. Fields years earlier, and together we went to a rehearsal studio, hired a pianist, and started to work on his movements.

"Frank was a quick learner and in only four days, he was a different man.

'How much do I owe you,' he said. 'Name it, I'll pay it.'

"I told him he could pay the dollar a day I had charged all the students of my dancing school.

'A dollar a day?' said Sinatra. 'I thought you'd ask at least a thousand a day.' He laughed and wrote out a cheque for four dollars, a cheque I never paid into my bank and somewhere still have among my souvenirs.

"We sat down in my suite at the Waldorf and I told him I had read stories recently about girls throwing panties on the stage at the New York Paramount Theatre where he was appearing. The story said they had the donors' names and phone numbers scribbled on in ink. I said that happened to me thirty-seven years earlier, but my thrower was classier, she had embroidered her name and address on the panties.

"He looked at me with a sly grin.

'That's a brilliant idea,' he said, 'I'll ask my publicists to see if they can find someone who can embroider.'

"Then he was gone, and I never saw him again. But less than a month later I read a story in some newspaper or other that Frank Sinatra was now getting panties thrown on the stage that had the donors' names and telephone numbers embroidered on the garments in silk."

There was an interesting sequel the following spring. "I received a call from a firm of accountants who were handling Frank Sinatra's ever increasing wealth.

'Mr. Brian,' said the accountant, 'We are unable to balance Mr. Sinatra's tax returns. Would you please pay into your bank account the four dollar cheque he paid for your dancing lessons. And perhaps you could send us a receipt for it. We can't find one in Mr. Sinatra's files. We would appreciate your cooperation.'

"I told them that so far as I was concerned they would never balance their books, for I planned to keep the cheque as a memento of a great performer. The caller didn't know what to say so I just hung up."

Frank Sinatra

Donald Brian returned next day to Hollywood to find the William Morris office had lots of parts for him to play.

"MGM gives me the most work," he said, "but I doubt if anything I do here will be remembered in a few years' time." His roles totalled in excess of one hundred, but few are recorded in Hollywood's history books.

Early in 1944, the Brian family got together and decided that the sunshine of California was not what they wanted for the rest of their lives.

"We have made a decision to sell our Bedford Drive house and head back east to stay in New York at our home in Great Neck," he told the *Los Angeles Examiner*.

"When we moved out to California, I had to close my dancing school and I miss the young people I met through the training. I will reopen the school when I return home and that will be my total dedication for the rest of my life."

Actor Robert Taylor, who had visited the Brians' Bedford Drive home as a guest, heard they were selling and offered what Donny and Virginia thought was an overly generous price for the property.

"But Sid Olcott told us that the price of houses in Beverly Hills had almost tripled since we bought the place in 1934, so we accepted Bob Taylor's offer and he wrote us out a cheque on the spot."

23 Dancing School Reopened

Back in New York, the Brians decided that they would build a dancing school with separate dormitories for boys and girls on the grounds of their Great Neck home.

Walter Winchell said this in his column in the *New York Times*:

"One of the all-time great performers to appear on the Broadway stage is coming home. He doesn't intend to seek work, and he'll forgive me telling you he is sixty-nine years old.

"But that isn't too old for Donald Brian to reopen the dancing school that made many young dancers, including his own wife Virginia O'Brien, into stars on Broadway.

"The new school will have live-in quarters for six girls and six boys so potential dancers can be accepted from all over North America.

"If you are interested you can write to Donald Brian at this newspaper and I will guarantee every letter will be handed to him personally."

Two weeks later Walter Winchell wrote another column about Donald Brian.

"Today I personally handed over three bags of mail to Mr. Brian. They have come from every corner of the United States and my secretary has counted more than 600 letters. More are still coming in to my office.

"Mr. Brian has hired a builder to construct his new dancing school and it will be ready in about three months. In the meantime, Mr. Brian will read every letter you sent to him and somehow will choose from all those applicants the very first students for his school.

"I want to assure parents that if their young dancers are chosen to work with Mr. Brian and his wife Virginia (she was once one of his students) that they will be well looked after and in a home that has, says their sixteen year old daughter Denise, never known a cross word or a word spoken in anger.

"Donny and Virginia have hired a cook to provide the best possible meals for every student and security guards who will keep the grounds safe twenty-four hours a day. Parents who come to see how their youngsters are doing will be guests of the Brians in their mansion at Great Neck.

"How much is this going to cost each student? A hundred, perhaps a thousand or maybe thousands of dollars a year? No! Students will be given the benefit of the Brians' superb knowledge of dancing, and singing too, for those with extra potential in that field, for one dollar a season. One dollar! You heard me right. The young people will be driven every day to a nearby private school for their regular education and the Brians are paying for this too.

"I can't begin to imagine how much all this is costing the Brians, because they refuse to tell me, but I quote from Virginia this one comment. 'Donny wants to end his life giving back more to the theatre than it ever gave him. Money will never be a consideration for accepting or refusing a student.'

"New York theatre has many big-hearted men and women like George M. Cohan who gave Donny Brian his first professional opportunity. These people contribute quietly, but generously to many people in need of assistance."

Walter Winchell concluded, "But this enormous explosion of generosity from the Brians surpasses everything anyone else in the New York theatre has ever given in the past."

A story in the *New York Times* late in 1944 announced the opening of the Donald and Virginia Brian School of Dancing. There were pictures of the dance studio, the dormitories and some of the students.

The story told how the Brians, with the aid of dancing schools around the United States, were able to select their first twelve resident students. In addition, they had accepted twenty more young dancers from the New York area who were near enough to Great Neck to travel back and forth from their homes for the lessons.

To make their general education program workable, all thirty-two students were either eleven or twelve years of age.

Three years later, in 1947, the *New York Post* said, "The remarkable seventy-two year old Donald Brian is continuing to work daily with his school of dancing." It added, "More than twelve of the original youngsters enrolled three years earlier were already working in the New York professional theatre in such productions as *Peter Pan* and other shows where children are needed."

Every Christmas the Brians rented a local community hall so their students could show what they had learned to their parents, friends and local residents.

On December 22, 1948, seventy-three year old Donald Brian decided to go onstage himself at the Christmas concert. He, and four of the students, had created a dance routine, and they had pleaded with him to appear at the concert.

You're a Girl I'd Like to Know was specially written for the occasion. Frederick Howard wrote the lyrics, Zoel Parenteau the music. The four students chosen to appear with Donald Brian were Suzanne Cook, Carol Dailey, Beverly Bender and Patricia Hansen.

When Donny Brian walked onstage the audience gave him a standing ovation.

In 2001, his daughter Denise remembered the night very clearly. "I was twenty then, working one of the spotlights when he came offstage," she said. "I had watched him doing steps he must have done when he was forty years younger. The tiredness I had noticed earlier in the day seemed to have vanished. There were tears streaming down his face as he turned once more to take a bow to the audience that was still standing and applauding.

'They still remember me,' he said to me. 'Isn't that wonderful?'

"He collapsed into a chair beside the stage and beckoned to mother, 'Take me home please. I'm very tired.'

"Mother drove him home in our car, and when I arrived home an hour later, having made sure all the students were in the bus to go back to the school, he was already in bed.

"I went upstairs to kiss him goodnight and he smiled that wonderful smile that had captivated audiences on Broadway and around North America for almost four decades. Then he fell asleep and I left the room quietly.

"When he didn't come down for breakfast next morning, mother and I went up to see if he was unwell. He still had that wonderful smile on his face, but was no longer alive.

"During the night he had died quietly in his sleep.

"St. Patrick's Roman Catholic Cathedral in New York was packed to the doors for his funeral. Thousands more waited outside. Actors like W.C. Fields, Humphrey Bogart, Fred Astaire, and Bob Hope had flown in from Hollywood. Sid Olcott and his wife Val were there. I can't begin to list the important people who were present. Dad never did meet his ninth president, but President Harry Truman and his wife Bess were there to pay their respects.

"Mother had anticipated something like this and hired a team of security men to seek out our special friends and give them all cards with details on how to get to a fleet of cars, which would bring them to our home in Great Neck. President Truman was with Bob Hope when Bob was given his card with instructions. The president asked our security man if he too could come to the house and although he wasn't on the list because nobody had expected him, the security man gave him one without hesitation.

"There were more than a hundred people at the house that mother had filled with recorded music from the shows in which Dad had appeared. It was rather a joyous occasion since mother addressed all the guests telling them to be joyful that such a great career had ended so peacefully."

'My friends,' she said, 'Donny had a wonderful life, he has gone somewhere now that his talents and honesty will surely be appreciated. Be happy for him, he would want to see smiles not tears.'

"It was after midnight before the final guests left. Mother had told Sid Olcott and Val that they must stay the night and we sat around for a while remembering all the good times, many before I was even born.

"A month after the funeral, an invitation arrived at the house. It was a hand-written invitation for mother and I to visit the White House for two days as guests of President Harry and Bess Truman. Of course we went and were treated like kings.

'I wish your husband could have been with you,' said President Truman. 'This invitation was to show our respect for the many hours of pleasure he gave to the United States.'

When President Truman left the White House, he sent Virginia Brian a signed copy of the picture that had been taken of them with the Trumans during their Washington visit. He said he would not leave the original in Washington, but would take it to his home in Independence, Missouri, "where it will always be displayed and where both of you will be welcome at any time."

"Dad had made enough good investments to ensure that his dancing school could continue," said Denise. "We hired the best choreographers we could find, but without Dad it was soon obvious that it was not going to last. As students graduated, there were not enough waiting to take their places and in 1951, we closed the school for the last time.

"I always remember someone telling me the day after the funeral that all the lights on Broadway's theatres were turned off for a minute in recognition of Dad's service to the American theatre. I wish I could have seen that, it was a perfect last salute for the King of Broadway."

Epilogue

Donald Brian had no secrets from anyone, at least none that needed hiding. His life was an open book. He had many friends and if he had enemies, nobody could name one.

But Denise Brian, his proud daughter, told me in 2001 the one secret he shared only with two people, his wife Virginia and her.

"My dad never became an American citizen," she said. "Many years ago, when I was about eighteen, I saw his passport lying on a table in his room. I picked it up and realised it was not American, but a British passport.

"He only travelled twice outside the United States. He had obtained the passport I looked at so that he and my mother could travel to England on their honeymoon. It was so old that it had expired eight years earlier.

"When Bob Hope asked him to fly to England to entertain the troops I can only guess that nobody asked for the passports of entertainers 'off to war.'

"I remember asking him why he had never become an American citizen since he had been so successful in the country he adopted. His answer was very simple. He said:

'If you are born a citizen of a country, wherever that country may be in the world, you should remain loyal to that country for the rest of your life. I love Newfoundland, which is a part of the British Empire, and I would be a traitor had I relinquished that citizenship.

'I gave in every way I could to the people of the United States, which had given me fame and wealth, but it did not give me birth and that is where my allegiance will always lie. I am a British subject and will die a British subject.'"

Donald Brian: The King of Broadway

Denise Brian still had the old British passport in her possession when we talked in 2001.

"Although I will likely never see St. John's, the city where he was born," she said, "I too feel an allegiance to the place that somehow taught him to be the wonderful caring man he remained every day of his life.

"What there is in the people of Newfoundland that made him the great person he remained throughout his life I do not know, but if you want a perfect description of Donald Brian you would simply have to say, 'He was a gentle man and a gentleman all his life, and everyone loved him for that.'"

She added one more important fact about Donny Brian. "Throughout his entire career he never missed a single performance through illness or for any other reason. He is the perfect example of the phrase 'The Show Must Go On!'"

Donald Brian, left, called this picture of himself with Billy Ryan, his best friend and tap dancing partner, the photograph he hoped he would never lose. It was taken in St. John's, Newfoundland, in 1890, when both boys were just 15. It travelled with him around the United States and to England with the Bob Hope armed forces show. It was in a frame at his bedside when he died in 1948.

By 1905 Donald Brian had become a popular nightclub entertainer in New York. When he began getting mail requesting autographed photographs he had this picture taken to send out to his fans.

When he appeared on Broadway again in 1906 with another George M. Cohan production, *Forty-five Minutes from Broadway*, this publicity picture was distributed to the daily newspapers in New York City.

In 1907 when Donald Brian was crowned the King of Broadway in *The Merry Widow*, this was the poster that appeared on billboards around New York. Two weeks after the show opened producer Henry Savage put a white strip across the centre of every poster that read, Starring Donald Brian, The King of Broadway.

Donald Brian as Prince Danilo in *The Merry Widow*, the production that made him a star. Henry Savage sent this picture to every weekly magazine across the United States. Records show it was published in at least 85 different magazines.

Donald Brian, as Prince Danilo, with Ethel Jackson, who played Sonia, the widow, in *The Merry Widow*.

Most cartoons in New York papers in1907 were directed at political or sports figures in the news. This cartoon published in the *New York Evening World* on November 2, 1907, two weeks after the musical's opening night, is believed to be the first cartoon to feature Broadway entertainers. The immense success of *The Merry Widow* earned it the right to this honour. Donald Brian and Ethel Jackson are shown centre, surrounded by other members of the cast, Lois Ewell, as Natalie who later took over the role of Sonia; R.E. Graham, as Popoff; Eva Bennett, as Fi-Fi; Frances Cameron, as Olga; Fred Fear, as Niche; and Jean Ward as Frou-Frou.

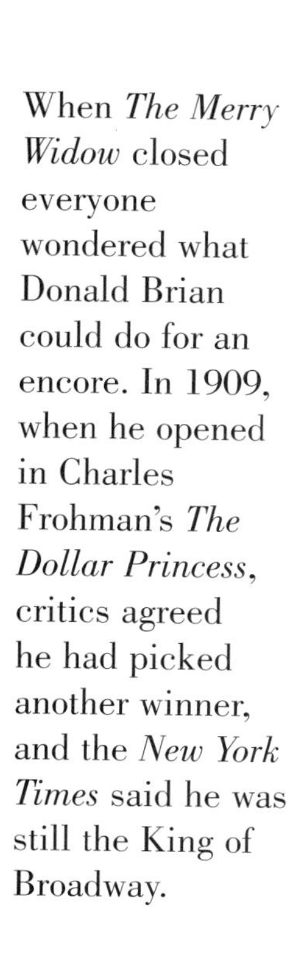

When *The Merry Widow* closed everyone wondered what Donald Brian could do for an encore. In 1909, when he opened in Charles Frohman's *The Dollar Princess*, critics agreed he had picked another winner, and the *New York Times* said he was still the King of Broadway.

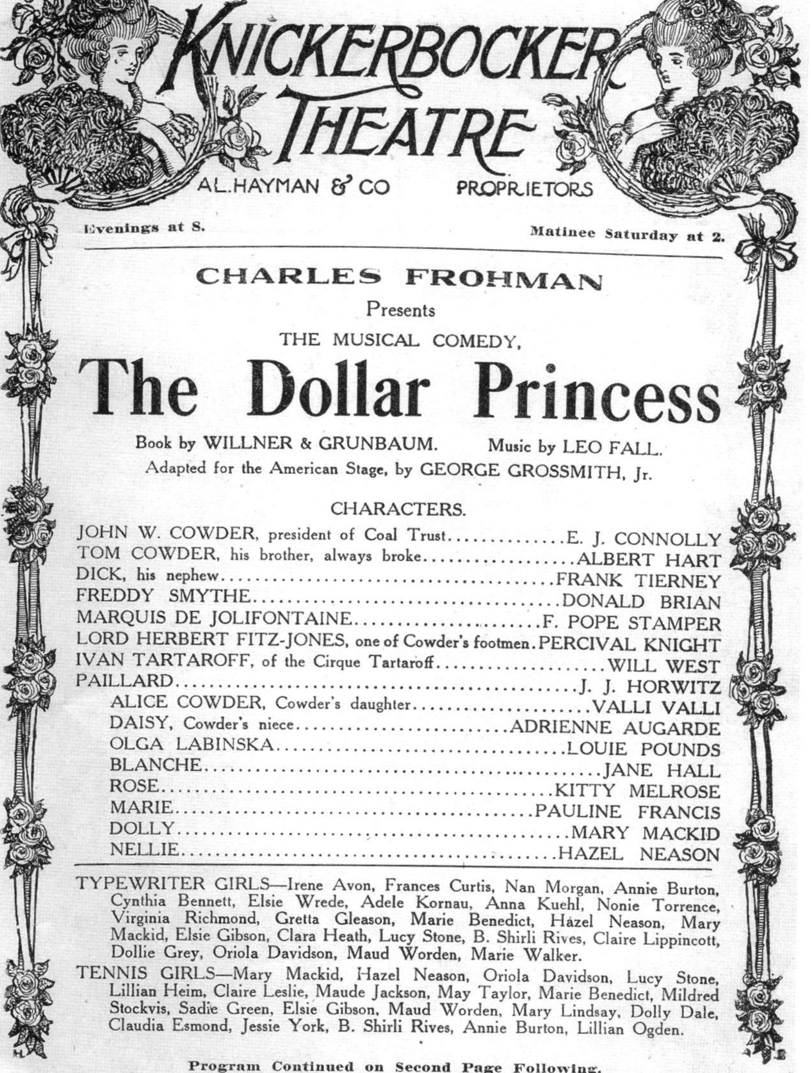

KNICKERBOCKER THEATRE

AL. HAYMAN & CO PROPRIETORS

Evenings at 8. Matinee Saturday at 2.

CHARLES FROHMAN

Presents

THE MUSICAL COMEDY,

The Dollar Princess

Book by WILLNER & GRUNBAUM. Music by LEO FALL.

Adapted for the American Stage, by GEORGE GROSSMITH, Jr.

CHARACTERS.

JOHN W. COWDER, president of Coal Trust..............E. J. CONNOLLY
TOM COWDER, his brother, always broke..................ALBERT HART
DICK, his nephew......................................FRANK TIERNEY
FREDDY SMYTHE..DONALD BRIAN
MARQUIS DE JOLIFONTAINE.........................F. POPE STAMPER
LORD HERBERT FITZ-JONES, one of Cowder's footmen.PERCIVAL KNIGHT
IVAN TARTAROFF, of the Cirque Tartaroff.....................WILL WEST
PAILLARD..J. J. HORWITZ
ALICE COWDER, Cowder's daughter.....................VALLI VALLI
DAISY, Cowder's niece........................ADRIENNE AUGARDE
OLGA LABINSKA..............................LOUIE POUNDS
BLANCHE...JANE HALL
ROSE....................................KITTY MELROSE
MARIE.................................PAULINE FRANCIS
DOLLY......................................MARY MACKID
NELLIE....................................HAZEL NEASON

TYPEWRITER GIRLS—Irene Avon, Frances Curtis, Nan Morgan, Annie Burton, Cynthia Bennett, Elsie Wrede, Adele Kornau, Anna Kuehl, Nonie Torrence, Virginia Richmond, Gretta Gleason, Marie Benedict, Hazel Neason, Mary Mackid, Elsie Gibson, Clara Heath, Lucy Stone, B. Shirli Rives, Claire Lippincott, Dollie Grey, Oriola Davidson, Maud Worden, Marie Walker.

TENNIS GIRLS—Mary Mackid, Hazel Neason, Oriola Davidson, Lucy Stone, Lillian Heim, Claire Leslie, Maude Jackson, May Taylor, Marie Benedict, Mildred Stockvis, Sadie Green, Elsie Gibson, Maud Worden, Mary Lindsay, Dolly Dale, Claudia Esmond, Jessie York, B. Shirli Rives, Annie Burton, Lillian Ogden.

Program Continued on Second Page Following.

Donald Brian had another major success when he starred in *The Siren*, another Charles Frohman production. Two of the ladies who sought his favours in the show, Julia Sanderson, right, and Elizabeth Firth, left, helped make *The Siren* into another long-running hit.

"Between 1907 and 1920 I probably had more studio pictures taken of myself than any other Broadway actor," said Donald Brian in 1943. "But I never paid a cent to any photographer. I received requests to pose for photographers every day of the week. I was apparently so important at that time that they used my pictures to show that Donald Brian had been in their studio as proof of their own talents."

Donald Brian said the musical, *The Girl from Utah*, another Charles Frohman production, was perhaps his most enjoyable memory of Broadway. “I was joined by Julia Sanderson and Joseph Cawthorne, two of Broadway’s biggest stars and two of the nicest people ever to grace the New York stage. Every performance was a delight.”

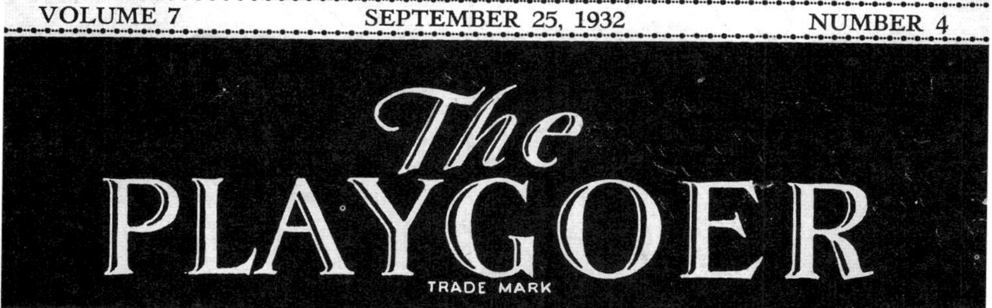

The only picture of Donald Brian and his wife Virginia O'Brien ever used together in the same show. His final appearance as Prince Danilo was in the 1931/32 production. Would you believe this youthful Donald Brian was 57 years old?
The Playgoer is the program cover for the Cass Theatre in Detroit, where the show played for one week on its national tour. It was only the second time Donald Brian and his wife starred together in the same show.

In 1934 Donald Brian appeared in a western film, *The Desert Trail*, with John Wayne at the Monogram Studio in Hollywood. Wayne later wrote in an article printed in the *Los Angeles Examiner* that had it not been for the encouragement and coaching in acting he received from Donald Brian during the filming he might never have become a big name in motion pictures. At the end of the shooting Wayne convinced the producers to give the costume shown to Donald Brian with a request that he be hired to appear in every one of his future films. While in Hollywood between 1934 and 1943 Brian appeared in thirty-four Wayne westerns and the film still remembered today, *Stage Coach*.

25 years ago today

RETURNS FROM TRIP TO ENGLAN
AND FRANCE.

DONALD BRIAN,
IN "THE GIRL BEHIND THE GUN",
WITH WILDA BENNETT, ADA MEADE;
AND JACK HAZZARD.

JAMES HAMILTON LEWIS.
SENATOR FROM ILLINOIS, SAYS
ENEMY FEARS THE UNITED
STATES — YANKEE DEEDS
FILL GERMAN PEOPLE WITH
WONDER AND TERROR.

SURGEON GENERAL
GORGAS REPORTS
A WAVE OF SPANISH
INFLUENZA SWEEP-
ING THROUGH OUR
ARMY CAMPS.

FRANKLIN D. ROOSEVELT.
ASSISTANT SECRETARY OF THE NAVY, RETURNED FROM VISIT
TO ENGLAND AND FRANCE — ILL WITH PNEUMONIA — AILMENT
CONTRACTED DURING RETURN VOYAGE — SUPPOSED TO HAVE DE-
VELOPED FROM SPANISH FLU.

9-21-43

Donald Brian's impact on the Broadway stage was never forgotten. In a syndicated feature, 25 Years Ago Today, printed in the *New York Times* in 1943, his appearance in *The Girl Behind The Gun*, in 1918, was still considered a memorable moment from that era.

Donald Brian's last photograph was taken in 1946. Would you believe this eternally youthful performer was 71 years old?

On December 22, 1948, Donald Brian made his last public appearance. This is part of the program presented by the students of his dancing school on that day. Frederick Howard and Zoel Parenteau wrote the last item on the program, *You're A Girl I'd like To Know*, featuring the top four dancers of the year, when the students convinced their teacher to dance once more on stage. Only a few hours later he died in his sleep at home.

ACT II.

THE RED MAN'S CALL

by Dorothy MacArdle

SCENE—Interior of a hut in a forest on a night of a storm in ancient Iceland.

CHARACTERS—

Children of the King	Nessa	Elaine Dailey
	Brendan	Jacqueline Benson
	Aideen	Denise Brian
	Laery	Elaine Nassiter
	Eilish	Adrienne Adelman
	Graina	Harolding Hunt
	Conn	Helen Hunt
	Sheila	Patricia Bradley
The Lilter		Donald Brian
The Red Man of the Sidhe — a piper		George Cowan

Alice Blue Gown .... Beverly Bender

DANCE OF THE HOURS

from La Gioconda

Morning	Adrienne Adelman Elaine Nassiter Suzanne Nassiter
Day	Patricia Hansen Jane McConaughy
Evening	Beverly Bender Elaine Dailey Lois Pfaff
Night	Jacqueline Benson Nancy W'rtenburg Denise Brian

Special Number

WILLIAM BENDER and GEORGE COWAN

THE BOND BETWEEN

by Mae Barry

SCENE—An upstairs sitting room in the Governor's home.

TIM:—A few minutes before ten p. m. The present.

CHARACTERS—

Mrs. Haledon	Suzanne Cook
Miss Brigg	Beverly Bender
Joan	Patricia Hansen
Mrs. Carson	Carol Keyser

YOU'RE A GIRL I'D LIKE TO KNOW

Musical Comedy Number

Lyrics - Frederick Howard

Music - Zoel Parenteau

Suzanne Cook — Beverly Bender

Carol Dailey — Patricia Hansen

Donald Brian

This number was written especially for this performance.

Index

Charles Foster met Donald Brian
for the first time in 1943 while on
leave from pilot training for the Royal British
Air Force in Calgary, Alberta.
Through his connection with silent film era director,
Sidney Olcott and his wife, Valentine,
Charles had the fortune to meet many of
Hollywood's most recognisable stars.
Charles lives in Riverview, New Brunswick.